Building Custom PHP Extensions

Blake Schwendiman

Copyright

Trademarks

The author has made every reasonable attempt to credit the appropriate trademark and/or registered trademark holders throughout this document.

Windows is a registered trademark of Microsoft Corporation in the United States and other countries.

Developer-friendly Request

If you have received a copy of this document electronically and you have not paid for it, please consider purchasing a licensed copy. A great deal of time and effort went into the creation of this document and if it has provided you with any useful information, visit http://www.php4devguide.com/ for details on purchasing this document. The more developers who support this type of documentation, the better the documentation will become.

About the Author

I don't have a lot to say about myself. I develop primarily in PHP, C and Delphi. I wrote this document because I thought it was a good idea.

Visit http://www.php4devguide.com/ to participate in online discussions and to get updates to this document as they become available.

Building Custom PHP Extensions

Motivation for this Document

In the recent past, I have been involved in various projects requiring either the creation of new PHP extensions or the editing of existing PHP extensions. While there is some documentation on how to do these tasks, I have found the documentation to be incomplete, difficult to find, out of date or a combination of the three. This document is an effort to centralize by own notes and to (hopefully) provide a tool from which other developers can benefit.

Motivation for Creating Your Own PHP Extension

Most PHP developers will not need to develop their own custom extension. PHP is a rich programming environment which is constantly updated through a strong open source development community. However, there are times when developing a custom extension may be necessary. Additionally, understanding the extension mechanism in PHP can provide a broader general understanding of PHP itself.

I have written two custom extensions with practical benefits in the very recent past. The first was written to map some proprietary C-based financial code into PHP for an example Intranet-based web site. The second was an implementation of a TNEF mail attachment decoder for a web-based email project.

Because of the nature of this document, it is assumed that the reader already has an understanding of PHP development, has built PHP from source and has a C programming background. You should also be familiar with PHP and its relationship to the Zend engine. Much of this document assumes you understand the relationship and so I often do not differentiate between the two in this text. This is an advanced topic not typical to general PHP programming.

Getting Started

The very first step in developing a new custom extension is to first download and build PHP from its source. The beginning of this document will focus on building PHP and the new extension on a Linux system. Later, the Windows build mechanism will be addressed.

Once you have extracted the PHP source and built it once to ensure that your system supports the tools needed for a plain-vanilla PHP build, it becomes time to focus on your new custom extension. To begin, we will develop a simple extension to show the process and then later build a complex extension to elaborate the internals and features available to extension builders.

First PHP Extension

Building the Shell

Navigate to the PHP installation directory, then to the **ext** directory. For example:

```
1    cd /path/to/php-4.x.x/ext
```

Run the *ext_skel* script in that directory with no parameters. This is the script that will create the initial files for a new PHP extension. Its parameters are shown in the table below.

--extname=module	module is the name of your extension
--proto=file	file contains prototypes of functions to create
--stubs=file	Leave out also all module specific stuff and write just function stubs with function value declarations and passed argument handling, and function entries and definitions at the end of the file, for copying and pasting into an already existing module.
--xml	generate xml documentation to be added to phpdoc-cvs
--skel=dir	path to the skeleton directory
--full-xml	generate xml documentation for a self-contained extension (not yet implemented)
--no-help	By default, ext_skel creates both comments in the source code and a test function to help first time module writers to get started and testing configuring and compiling their module. This option turns off all such things which may just annoy experienced PHP module coders. Especially useful with the --stubs parameter.

Table 1: Parameters to the ext_skel script.

> NOTE: I suggest you read the *README.EXT_SKEL* file in the main PHP install path for details about the script.

For our first extension, we will be creating some simple functions:

double **calcpi**(*int* iterations)

This function returns an approximation of pi. The algorithm is a simplistic random-number method of calculating pi which is neither efficient nor particularly accurate – but it is fun.

string **reverse**(*string* input)

This function returns the reverse version of a string. For example "Test String" becomes "gnirtS tseT".

array **uniquechars**(*string* input, [*bool* case_sensitive])

Returns an array of all the unique characters in the input string. For example "Test String" returns an array containing the elements 'T', 'e', 's', 't', 'S', 'r', 'i', 'n' and 'g'. The case_sensitive parameter which is optional and will be implicitly true sets a flag which affects whether the search for characters should be case sensitive. If case_sensitive is false, the previous example will return 't', 'e', 's', 'r', 'i', 'n' and 'g' – not including the uppercase/lowercase versions of the characters.

None of the above functions are particularly useful, but as examples of creating PHP extensions, they provide coverage of many of the features that will be used in a more complete extension.

First, create a text file containing the function prototypes. This file should contain one function prototype per line. For the example functions, the file should contain the following three lines (the last line may wrap in this view, but should not wrap in the actual file you create):

```
1    double calcpi( int iterations) Calculate Pi
2    string reverse( string input ) Reverse the
     input string
3    array uniquechars( string input [, bool
     case_sensitive] ) Return the unique
     characters in the input string
```

Code Fragment 1: Prototype file for first_test.

Call this file *first_test.proto*. The *ext_skel* script will read this file and parse it to build the skeleton C code for the extension. It is not necessary to build a prototype file, but doing so will greatly reduce the amount of actual C coding required to continue and will decrease the risk of incorrectly prototyping the C functions as required to work within the PHP framework.

Each line of the prototype file contains information about a function that will be visible within PHP. The format of each line is:

> [function return type] function name (parameter list) optional comment

The function return type is optional and has no effect on the generated skeleton code except in the internal documentation. The parameter list is a comma-separated list consisting of a type and a parameter name. Parameters may be optionally enclosed in square brackets signifying an optional parameter in the PHP context.

With the prototype file created, it is time to run the *ext_skel* script. Execute the script using:

```
1    cd /path/to/php/ext
2    ./ext_skel --extname=first_test --
     proto=first_test.proto
```

Assuming you have the correct write permissions for your system, the script will run and report a list of instructions required to now build and install the new extension. The steps are:

1. cd ..
2. vi ext/first_test/config.m4
3. ./buildconf
4. ./configure --[with | enable]-first_test
5. make
6. ./php -f ext/first_test/first_test.php
7. vi ext/first_test/first_test.c
8. make

I suggest following these steps almost verbatim to ensure that the extension properly builds and integrates into PHP. Before doing so, however, it is interesting to see the files that have been created in the */path/to/php/ext/first_test* directory. The files are:

config.m4	This file is used by the *buildconf* script later to integrate the new extension into the PHP *configure* script.
CREDITS	An essentially empty text file for you to credit yourself for your great work.
EXPERIMENTAL	An empty text file.
first_test.c	The implementation of the new extension.
first_test.php	A PHP test script for the new extension.
php_first_test.h	The header file of the new extension.
tests	A directory containing at least one PHP test file for use with the automated build testing command *make test*.

Table 2: Files generated by the ext_skel script.

The first working step required to build the new extension is to edit the config.m4 file. This file is used by *buildconf* to update the main PHP *configure* script. If you do not make any edits to this file, the execution of the *buildconf* script will result in no changes to the *configure* script at all. The config.m4 file is a Unix m4 macro file. More information about m4 can be found at http://www.gnu.org/software/m4/. All comments in the m4 file are denoted with **dnl**.

The config.m4 file created for the *first_test* extension is shown below.

```
1    dnl $Id$
2    dnl config.m4 for extension first_test
3
4    dnl Comments in this file start with the
     string 'dnl'.
5    dnl Remove where necessary. This file will
     not work
6    dnl without editing.
7
8    dnl If your extension references something
     external, use with:
9
10   dnl PHP_ARG_WITH(first_test, for first_test
     support,
11   dnl Make sure that the comment is aligned:
12   dnl [  --with-first_test          Include
     first_test support])
13
14   dnl Otherwise use enable:
15
16   dnl PHP_ARG_ENABLE(first_test, whether to
     enable first_test support,
17   dnl Make sure that the comment is aligned:
18   dnl [  --enable-first_test         Enable
     first_test support])
19
20   if test "$PHP_FIRST_TEST" != "no"; then
21     dnl Write more examples of tests here...
22
23     dnl # --with-first_test -> check with-path
24     dnl SEARCH_PATH="/usr/local /usr"     #
     you might want to change this
25     dnl SEARCH_FOR="/include/first_test.h"  #
     you most likely want to change this
```

```
26   dnl if test -r $PHP_FIRST_TEST/; then #
     path given as parameter
27   dnl    FIRST_TEST_DIR=$PHP_FIRST_TEST
28   dnl else # search default path list
29   dnl    AC_MSG_CHECKING([for first_test
     files in default path])
30   dnl    for i in $SEARCH_PATH ; do
31   dnl       if test -r $i/$SEARCH_FOR; then
32   dnl          FIRST_TEST_DIR=$i
33   dnl          AC_MSG_RESULT(found in $i)
34   dnl       fi
35   dnl    done
36   dnl fi
37   dnl
38   dnl if test -z "$FIRST_TEST_DIR"; then
39   dnl    AC_MSG_RESULT([not found])
40   dnl    AC_MSG_ERROR([Please reinstall the
     first_test distribution])
41   dnl fi
42
43   dnl # --with-first_test -> add include
     path
44   dnl
     PHP_ADD_INCLUDE($FIRST_TEST_DIR/include)
45
46   dnl # --with-first_test -> chech for lib
     and symbol presence
47   dnl LIBNAME=first_test # you may want to
     change this
48   dnl LIBSYMBOL=first_test # you most likely
     want to change this
49
50   dnl PHP_CHECK_LIBRARY($LIBNAME,$LIBSYMBOL,
51   dnl [
52   dnl    PHP_ADD_LIBRARY_WITH_PATH($LIBNAME,
     $FIRST_TEST_DIR/lib,
     FIRST_TEST_SHARED_LIBADD)
53   dnl    AC_DEFINE(HAVE_FIRST_TESTLIB,1,[ ])
54   dnl ],[
55   dnl    AC_MSG_ERROR([wrong first_test lib
     version or lib not found])
56   dnl ],[
57   dnl    -L$FIRST_TEST_DIR/lib -lm -ldl
58   dnl ])
59   dnl
60   dnl PHP_SUBST(FIRST_TEST_SHARED_LIBADD)
61
62   PHP_NEW_EXTENSION(first_test,
     first_test.c, $ext_shared)
63   fi
```

Code Fragment 2: Unedited config.m4 file after running ext_skel.

The lines that must be changed are lines 16 and 18 above. The only changes required are that the comments must be removed. The same file from above, with the appropriate edits is shown below.

```
1.   dnl $Id$
2    dnl config.m4 for extension first_test
3
4    dnl Comments in this file start with the
     string 'dnl'.
5    dnl Remove where necessary. This file will
     not work
6    dnl without editing.
7
8    dnl If your extension references something
     external, use with:
9
10   dnl PHP_ARG_WITH(first_test, for first_test
     support,
11   dnl Make sure that the comment is aligned:
12   dnl [  --with-first_test          Include
     first_test support])
13
14   dnl Otherwise use enable:
15
16   PHP_ARG_ENABLE(first_test, whether to enable
     first_test support,
17   dnl Make sure that the comment is aligned:
18   [  --enable-first_test          Enable
     first_test support])
19
20   if test "$PHP_FIRST_TEST" != "no"; then
21     dnl Write more examples of tests here...
22
23     dnl # --with-first_test -> check with-path
24     dnl SEARCH_PATH="/usr/local /usr"     #
     you might want to change this
25     dnl SEARCH_FOR="/include/first_test.h"  #
     you most likely want to change this
26     dnl if test -r $PHP_FIRST_TEST/; then #
     path given as parameter
27     dnl   FIRST_TEST_DIR=$PHP_FIRST_TEST
28     dnl else # search default path list
29     dnl   AC_MSG_CHECKING([for first_test
     files in default path])
30     dnl   for i in $SEARCH_PATH ; do
31     dnl     if test -r $i/$SEARCH_FOR; then
32     dnl       FIRST_TEST_DIR=$i
33     dnl       AC_MSG_RESULT(found in $i)
34     dnl     fi
35     dnl   done
36     dnl fi
```

```
37   dnl
38   dnl if test -z "$FIRST_TEST_DIR"; then
39   dnl   AC_MSG_RESULT([not found])
40   dnl   AC_MSG_ERROR([Please reinstall the
     first_test distribution])
41   dnl fi
42
43   dnl # --with-first_test -> add include
     path
44   dnl
     PHP_ADD_INCLUDE($FIRST_TEST_DIR/include)
45
46   dnl # --with-first_test -> chech for lib
     and symbol presence
47   dnl LIBNAME=first_test # you may want to
     change this
48   dnl LIBSYMBOL=first_test # you most likely
     want to change this
49
50   dnl PHP_CHECK_LIBRARY($LIBNAME,$LIBSYMBOL,
51   dnl [
52   dnl   PHP_ADD_LIBRARY_WITH_PATH($LIBNAME,
     $FIRST_TEST_DIR/lib,
     FIRST_TEST_SHARED_LIBADD)
53   dnl   AC_DEFINE(HAVE_FIRST_TESTLIB,1,[ ])
54   dnl ],[
55   dnl   AC_MSG_ERROR([wrong first_test lib
     version or lib not found])
56   dnl ],[
57   dnl   -L$FIRST_TEST_DIR/lib -lm -ldl
58   dnl ])
59   dnl
60   dnl PHP_SUBST(FIRST_TEST_SHARED_LIBADD)
61
62   PHP_NEW_EXTENSION(first_test,
     first_test.c, $ext_shared)
63 fi
```

Code Fragment 3: Edited config.m4 for the first_test example project.

```
64   NOTE: The buildconf script requires recent
     versions of  autoconf, automake and libtool.
     If your system does not have the required
     versions of these tools you must download
     and install them to continue.
```

libtool	http://www.gnu.org/software/libtool/
automake	http://www.gnu.org/software/automake/automake.html
autoconf	http://www.gnu.org/software/autoconf/

Table 3: External software required by the buildconf script.

The next step is to execute the *buildconf* script. Recently the *buildconf* script has been changed so that it cannot be run accidentally against a non-development version of PHP. If you attempt to run *buildconf* using a recent version of the script, you will likely receive the warning message, "You should not run buildconf in a release package. Use buildconf --force to override this check."

If you receive this warning, simply run ./*buildconf force* to avoid the warning. I suggest backing up your current copy of the *configure* script before running *buildconf* for the first time. Once the *buildconf* script is finished, you can check that the new PHP *configure* script has the new extension information with the command, "./*configure help*" which lists all the configuration options. Grep for the name of the new extension to ensure that it is included in the *configure* script.

It is now possible to configure, build and test PHP with the new extension. Execute the following commands to do so:

1. ./configure --enable-first_test
2. make
3. ./sapi/cli/php -f ext/first_test/first_test.php

> NOTE: The above commands are steps 4, 5 and 6 that were provided by the *ext_skel* script, modified for this example and for changes in the location of the PHP binaries.

Upon executing the script (line 3), if all has gone well, you will receive a congratulatory message such as the following:

Functions available in the test extension:
confirm_first_test_compiled
calcpi
reverse
uniquechars

Congratulations! You have successfully
modified ext/first_test/config.m4. Module
first_test is now compiled into PHP.

However, if you try to call any of the functions in the
new extension, you'll get a warning message. For
example:

echo '<? calcpi(10); ?>' | ./sapi/cli/php

Results in:

Warning: calcpi: not yet implemented in - on
line 1

This is due to the fact that none of the functions
actually have an implementation. That's the next step
in the process.

Implementing the Extension

So far, we haven't examined the source or header files
that were created by the *ext_skel* script. Now it's time
to dive in and make them useful. The header file is a
very standard PHP extension header file and requires
no modification for this particular extension. The
header file will be revisited in the full example later in
this document.

The implementation file, *first_test.c*, must be edited to provide the desired functionality. To begin, locate the implementation of the *calcpi* function. Initially, the implementation looks like the following:

```
1   /* {{{ proto double calcpi(int iterations)
2      Calculate Pi */
3   PHP_FUNCTION(calcpi)
4   {
5       int argc = ZEND_NUM_ARGS();
6       long iterations;
7
8       if (zend_parse_parameters(argc
    TSRMLS_CC, "l", &iterations) == FAILURE)
9           return;
10
11      php_error(E_WARNING, "calcpi: not yet
    implemented");
12  }
13  /* }}} */
```

Code Fragment 4: Unedited implementation of the calcpi() function.

Lines 1, 2 and 13 are comments that provide some human readable breaks and documentation within the source. Line 3 is the function prototype, simplified by a C macro. Lines 5 and 6 declare some required local variables and line 11 is the line that provides the warning message indicating that the function is not yet implemented. The most valuable line that was automatically generated is line 8. This single line is the function that ensures that the parameters passed from the PHP script are consistent with the function prototype and then populates the local C variables appropriately. This function will be discussed in greater detail later.

To make this function actually do what we want, we must provide a real implementation and remove the extraneous warning. Using a simplistic PI calculation algorithm, the function becomes:

```
1   /* {{{ proto double calcpi(int iterations)
2       Calculate Pi */
3   PHP_FUNCTION(calcpi)
4   {
5           int argc = ZEND_NUM_ARGS();
6           long iterations;
7           int index, hits;
8           double randx, randy, distance, value;
9
10          if (zend_parse_parameters(argc
    TSRMLS_CC, "l", &iterations) == FAILURE)
11              return;
12
13
14          hits = 0;
15          for ( index = 0; index < iterations;
    index++ )
16          {
17              randx = rand();
18              randy = rand();
19
20              randx /= RAND_MAX;
21              randy /= RAND_MAX;
22
23              distance = sqrt( ( randx * randx ) + (
    randy * randy ) );
24
25              if ( distance <= 1.0 )
26              {
27                  hits++;
28              }
29              value = ( (double) hits / (double)
    index );
30              value *= 4.0;
31          }
32
33          value  = ( (double) hits / (double)
    iterations );
34          value *= 4.0;
35          RETVAL_DOUBLE( value );
36  }
37  /* }}} */
```

**Code Fragment 5: Full implementation of the calcpi()
function.**

As can be seen from the above code, the warning
message has been removed and a simple PI
calculation algorithm has been added. The most
significant change from the extension perspective is

line 35, which assigns the return value and indicates its type as DOUBLE.

Now calling the function:

> echo '<? print(calcpi(10000) . "\n"); ?>' | ./sapi/cli/php

Returns the following (or similar, based on the calculated value):

> 3.15

The implementation for the *reverse* function is below. Note that none of the implementations for this test extension are to be considered models for efficient C programming.

```
1   /* {{{ proto string reverse(string input)
2      Reverse the input string */
3   PHP_FUNCTION(reverse)
4   {
5       char *input = NULL;
6       int argc = ZEND_NUM_ARGS();
7       int input_len;
8       char* workstr;
9       int index;
10
11      if (zend_parse_parameters(argc
    TSRMLS_CC, "s", &input, &input_len) ==
    FAILURE)
12          return;
13
14      workstr = (char*) emalloc( input_len + 1
    );
15      memset( workstr, 0, input_len + 1 );
16      for ( index = 0; index < input_len;
    index++ )
17      {
18          workstr[index] = input[input_len - (
    index + 1 )];
19      }
20
21      RETVAL_STRING( workstr, 1 );
22
23      efree( workstr );
```

```
24  }
25  /* }}} */
```

**Code Fragment 6: Implementation of the reverse()
function.**

This function demonstrates two things. First, this
function demonstrates using the **emalloc** and **efree**
memory management routines in place of the
standard C **malloc/free** functions. These memory
management routines are preferred when developing
PHP extensions as they allow the Zend engine to
manage the entire memory pool which allows the
engine to determine when a block is in use and
automatically free unused blocks and blocks with lost
references, preventing memory leaks. There are
several more memory management routines available
for your use, all of which will be discussed later.

The second concept demonstrated in the above
example is how to return a string to PHP. The
RETVAL_STRING macro accepts two parameters,
the string itself (character pointer) and a Boolean flag
indicating whether or not to duplicate the string using
estrdup. In the above example, I allocate the
memory for a working buffer, create the reversed
string and then set the return value using the flag to
duplicate the string. Lastly, I free the working buffer.

Alternately, I could have simply allocated the working
buffer and returned it directly without duplication,
but I personally feel it is better to free memory I
allocate for internal use and let the Zend engine deal
with freeing its own internal memory allocation that
results from using the RETVAL_STRING macro as I
did above. That said, if I were absolutely interested in
performance, I would eliminate the additional

memory allocation and buffer copying and simply note my reasoning in the code.

The implementation of the *uniquechars* function is below.

```
1   /* {{{ proto array uniquechars(string input
    [, bool case_sensitive])
2       Return the unique characters in the input
    string */
3   PHP_FUNCTION(uniquechars)
4   {
5       char *input = NULL;
6       int argc = ZEND_NUM_ARGS();
7       int input_len;
8       zend_bool case_sensitive;
9       char* workbuf;
10      int index, work_index;
11
12      if (zend_parse_parameters(argc
    TSRMLS_CC, "s|b", &input, &input_len,
    &case_sensitive) == FAILURE)
13          return;
14
15      if ( argc == 1 )
16      {
17          case_sensitive = 1;
18      }
19
20
21      work_index = 0;
22      workbuf = (char*) emalloc( input_len + 1
    );
23      memset( workbuf, 0, input_len + 1 );
24      for ( index = 0; index < input_len;
    index++ )
25      {
26          if ( case_sensitive )
27          {
28              if ( !strchr( workbuf, input[index]
    ) )
29              {
30                  workbuf[work_index] =
    input[index];
31                  work_index++;
32              }
33          }
34          else
35          {
36              if ( !strchr( workbuf, tolower(
    input[index] ) ) )
37              {
```

```
38              workbuf[work_index] = tolower(
   input[index] );
39              work_index++;
40          }
41        }
42      }
43
44      array_init( return_value );
45      for ( index = 0; index < input_len;
   index++ )
46      {
47        if ( workbuf[index] != '\0' )
48        {
49          add_next_index_stringl(
   return_value, &workbuf[index], 1, 1 );
50        }
51      }
52
53      efree( workbuf );
54    }
55  /* }}} */
```

**Code Fragment 7: Implementation of the uniquechars()
function.**

The above function works by first creating a standard
C character array containing all of the unique
characters in lines 21 through 42. It sets the
case_sensitive flag to the default (true) in lines 15
through 18 if the parameter is not passed at all. The
really interesting code, though, is in lines 44 through
50 where the PHP array variable is created and
populated.

Line 44 initializes the return value as an array. In the
previous two examples, the *return_value* variable was
used opaquely in the RETVAL_XXX functions, but
it is important to note that every function that is
prototyped using the PHP_FUNCTION macro has a
standard return variable called *return_value*. It is
easiest to manipulate this value using the
RETVAL_XXX or RETURN_XXX macros, but
those macros do not provide array functionality.

Once the array variable is initialized, items are added to the array (in this example) using the *add_next_index_string* function. This function takes four parameters:

1. The array variable itself
2. A character pointer representing the string to add
3. The length of the string being added
4. Whether to duplicate the string being added

There are many array manipulation functions available, all of which are discussed in depth later in this document.

Now that the new extension is fully implemented, it becomes possible to test it in PHP. The following is a sample PHP script and the output generated by the script.

```php
1   <?php
2     print( 'Calculating PI using 10
      iterations: ' . calcpi( 10 ) . "\n" );
3     print( 'Calculating PI using 100
      iterations: ' . calcpi( 100 ) . "\n" );
4     print( 'Calculating PI using 1,000
      iterations: ' . calcpi( 1000 ) . "\n" );
5     print( 'Calculating PI using 10,000
      iterations: ' . calcpi( 10000 ) . "\n" );
6     print( 'Calculating PI using 100,000
      iterations: ' . calcpi( 100000 ) . "\n" );
7     print( "\n" );
8
9     print( 'Reverse of "Zend Engine" is "' .
      reverse( 'Zend Engine' ) . "\"\n" );
10    print( "\n" );
11
12    print( 'The unique characters in "Zend
      Engine" (case sensitive) are: ' . implode(
      ',', uniquechars( 'Zend Engine' ) ) . "\n"
      );
13    print( 'The unique characters in "Zend
      Engine" (case insensitive) are: ' . implode(
      ',', uniquechars( 'Zend Engine', false ) ) .
      "\n" );
```

```
14    print( "\n" );
15    ?>
```

Code Fragment 8: PHP script for testing the first_test extension.

```
1    Calculating PI using 10 iterations: 3.2
2    Calculating PI using 100 iterations: 3.2
3    Calculating PI using 1,000 iterations: 3.248
4    Calculating PI using 10,000 iterations:
     3.1356
5    Calculating PI using 100,000 iterations:
     3.1358
6
7    Reverse of "Zend Engine" is "enignE dneZ"
8
9    The unique characters in "Zend Engine" (case
     sensitive) are: Z,e,n,d, ,E,g,i
10   The unique characters in "Zend Engine" (case
     insensitive) are: z,e,n,d, ,g,i
```

Results/Output 1: Output of the test PHP script.

Summary

The simple example in the above sections shows how quickly one can begin developing custom PHP extensions. While the functions used in the example are neither useful nor particularly interesting, they do illustrate the mechanics of building PHP extensions and have provided the foundation for the next sections of this document. The next section provides as much detail as possible into the tools available for extension creation. Following that section, there is a complex extension implementation to illuminate as much of the toolset as possible.

Building Extensions – The Details

This section is dedicated to documenting the tools, APIs and macros involved in creating custom extensions. There is a great deal of information in this section that is illustrated in either the simple example above or in the complex example following this section. This section is intended to be the reference section of the document with as much detail provided as possible. However, some aspects of this section may not be completely clear outside the context of the examples. I recommend skimming this section, studying the examples and then returning to this section for details as needed.

ext_skel

The first tool, *ext_skel* was demonstrated in the previous section. However, not all of its command-line options were fully discussed. The command-line options are again listed below:

--extname=module	module is the name of your extension
--proto=file	file contains prototypes of functions to create
--stubs=file	Leave out also all module specific stuff and write just function stubs with function value declarations and passed argument handling, and function entries and definitions at the end of the file, for copying and pasting into an already existing module.
--xml	generate xml documentation to be added to phpdoc-cvs
--skel=dir	path to the skeleton directory
--full-xml	generate xml documentation for a self-contained extension (not yet implemented)

--no-help	By default, ext_skel creates both comments in the source code and a test function to help first time module writers to get started and testing configuring and compiling their module. This option turns off all such things which may just annoy experienced PHP module coders. Especially useful with the --stubs parameter.

Table 4: Parameters to the ext_skel script – revisited.

The options used in the above example did not include the **stubs, xml, skel, full xml** nor **no help**.

By specifying the **no help** option, the script will not generate the *<extension>.php* test script nor will the *<extension>.c* source file contain most of the comments that are generated automatically. This is intended to simplify the code for experienced extension writers.

The **xml** option causes the script to create an additional file, *<extension>.xml* which creates the basis of a phpdoc file. These files are used to automatically generate documentation on the PHP web site and can be used to generate other documentation files. The **full xml** option is not currently implemented.

The **skel** option indicates the path to the *skeleton* directory, or the path to the directory that contains the *skeleton* files. By default, the path is /path/to/php/ext/skeleton. The default path contains skeleton or template versions of all the files created by the *ext_skel* script. You may wish to change the base skeleton files or create your own in a new directory if you are writing several extensions.

By specifying the **stubs** option, you are indicating that the *ext_skel* script should write only the function stubs to the file specified in the parameter. The script will not create a new extension directory nor will it create any of the additional support files. This option is particularly useful if you are simply adding new functions to an existing extension. The entire output of the script when run against the prototype file in the previous example is:

```
1   /* {{{ proto double calcpi(int iterations)
2       Calculate Pi */
3   PHP_FUNCTION(calcpi)
4   {
5           int argc = ZEND_NUM_ARGS();
6           long iterations;
7
8           if (zend_parse_parameters(argc
    TSRMLS_CC, "l", &iterations) == FAILURE)
9                   return;
10
11          php_error(E_WARNING, "calcpi: not
    yet implemented");
12  }
13  /* }}} */
14
15  /* {{{ proto string reverse(string input)
16      Reverse the input string */
17  PHP_FUNCTION(reverse)
18  {
19          char *input = NULL;
20          int argc = ZEND_NUM_ARGS();
21          int input_len;
22
23          if (zend_parse_parameters(argc
    TSRMLS_CC, "s", &input, &input_len) ==
    FAILURE)
24                  return;
25
26          php_error(E_WARNING, "reverse: not
    yet implemented");
27  }
28  /* }}} */
29
30  /* {{{ proto array uniquechars(string input
    [, bool case_sensitive])
31      Return the unique characters in the input
    string */
32  PHP_FUNCTION(uniquechars)
33  {
```

```
34              char *input = NULL;
35              int argc = ZEND_NUM_ARGS();
36              int input_len;
37              zend_bool case_sensitive;
38
39              if (zend_parse_parameters(argc
     TSRMLS_CC, "s|b", &input, &input_len,
     &case_sensitive) == FAILURE)
40                      return;
41
42              php_error(E_WARNING, "uniquechars:
     not yet implemented");
43      }
44  /* }}} */
45
46
47  /* ------------------------------------------
     ------------------ */
48
49              PHP_FE(calcpi,   NULL)
50              PHP_FE(reverse,  NULL)
51              PHP_FE(uniquechars,     NULL)
52
53
54  /* ------------------------------------------
     ------------------ */
55
56  PHP_FUNCTION(calcpi);
57  PHP_FUNCTION(reverse);
58  PHP_FUNCTION(uniquechars);
```

Results/Output 2: Example output of ext_skel script using the   stubs option.

These lines can be easily cut and pasted into another extension implementation to add new functionality.

One aspect of the   **proto** option that was not covered above is types available in prototype definitions. The available type names are int, long, double, float, string, bool, boolean, array, object, resource, handle, mixed, void. The types int and long generate the same function stub. Also, double and float are considered the same as are bool and boolean and resource and handle.

The stubs code for checking the argument count is automatically generated in all cases. The code for assigning variables of type int, long, double, float, string, bool, boolean, object, mixed and array is also automatically generated. However, the types object, mixed and array are set to standard PHP zval pointers and must be manipulated using macros or functions described later in this section. The types handle and resource generate some stub code that cannot be compiled without modification, as illustrated in the examples below. The parsing script cannot correctly handle variable argument lists. It is important to always double-check any automatically generated code.

Below is a prototype file containing several example functions and below that is the stub code that was generated for those functions.

```
1   int func1( int arg1, long arg2, double arg3,
    float arg4 )
2   int func2( string arg1, bool, arg2, boolean
    arg3 )
3   int func3( array arg1 )
4   int func4( object arg1 )
5   int func5( resource arg1, handle arg2 )
6   int func6( mixed arg1 )
7   int func7( void )
```

Code Fragment 9: Example prototypes showing code generation for various PHP types.

```
1   /* {{{ proto int func1(int arg1, long arg2,
    double arg3, float arg4)
2       */
3   PHP_FUNCTION(func1)
4   {
5           int argc = ZEND_NUM_ARGS();
6           long arg1;
7           long arg2;
8           double arg3;
9           double arg4;
10
11          if (zend_parse_parameters(argc
    TSRMLS_CC, "lldd", &arg1, &arg2, &arg3,
    &arg4) == FAILURE)
12                  return;
```

```
13
14             php_error(E_WARNING, "func1: not yet
   implemented");
15 }
16 /* }}} */
17
18 /* {{{ proto int func2(string arg1, bool )
19     arg2, boolean arg3 ) */
20 PHP_FUNCTION(func2)
21 {
22         char *arg1 = NULL;
23         int argc = ZEND_NUM_ARGS();
24         int arg1_len;
25         zend_bool ;
26
27         if (zend_parse_parameters(argc
   TSRMLS_CC, "sb", &arg1, &arg1_len, &) ==
   FAILURE)
28                 return;
29
30         php_error(E_WARNING, "func2: not yet
   implemented");
31 }
32 /* }}} */
33
34 /* {{{ proto int func3(array arg1)
35     */
36 PHP_FUNCTION(func3)
37 {
38         int argc = ZEND_NUM_ARGS();
39         zval *arg1 = NULL;
40
41         if (zend_parse_parameters(argc
   TSRMLS_CC, "a", &arg1) == FAILURE)
42                 return;
43
44         php_error(E_WARNING, "func3: not yet
   implemented");
45 }
46 /* }}} */
47
48 /* {{{ proto int func4(object arg1)
49     */
50 PHP_FUNCTION(func4)
51 {
52         int argc = ZEND_NUM_ARGS();
53         zval *arg1 = NULL;
54
55         if (zend_parse_parameters(argc
   TSRMLS_CC, "o", &arg1) == FAILURE)
56                 return;
57
58         php_error(E_WARNING, "func4: not yet
   implemented");
59 }
```

```
60  /* }}} */
61
62  /* {{{ proto int func5(resource arg1, handle
    arg2)
63      */
64  PHP_FUNCTION(func5)
65  {
66          int argc = ZEND_NUM_ARGS();
67          int arg1_id = -1;
68          int arg2_id = -1;
69          zval *arg1 = NULL;
70          zval *arg2 = NULL;
71
72          if (zend_parse_parameters(argc
    TSRMLS_CC, "rr", &arg1, &arg2) == FAILURE)
73                  return;
74
    if (arg1) {
75                  ZEND_FETCH_RESOURCE(???,
    ???, arg1, arg1_id, "???", ???_rsrc_id);
76          }
    if (arg2) {
77                  ZEND_FETCH_RESOURCE(???,
    ???, arg2, arg2_id, "???", ???_rsrc_id);
78          }
79
80          php_error(E_WARNING, "func5: not yet
    implemented");
81  }
82  /* }}} */
83
84  /* {{{ proto int func6(mixed arg1)
85      */
86  PHP_FUNCTION(func6)
87  {
88          int argc = ZEND_NUM_ARGS();
89          zval *arg1 = NULL;
90
91          if (zend_parse_parameters(argc
    TSRMLS_CC, "z", &arg1) == FAILURE)
92                  return;
93
94          php_error(E_WARNING, "func6: not yet
    implemented");
95  }
96  /* }}} */
97
98  /* {{{ proto int func7()
99      */
100 PHP_FUNCTION(func7)
101 {
102         if (ZEND_NUM_ARGS() != 0) {
103                 WRONG_PARAM_COUNT;
104         }
```

```
105         php_error(E_WARNING, "func7: not yet
    implemented");
106 }
107 /* }}} */
```

Code Fragment 10: C code illustrating code generated for various PHP types.

As can be seen from the above examples, most of the stub code is compilable and much of it is directly usable with little modification. However, lines 75 and 77 above contain non-compilable code as a side effect of using the resource or handle type. The ZEND_FETCH_RESOURCE macro will be described in detail later.

Memory Management Functions

When creating extensions for PHP, it is critical to use the engine's memory management functions instead of the standard C library's versions. Using the replacement functions ensures that the Zend engine is aware of memory allocations and deallocations and provides some safety against memory leaks. The memory management functions are listed below.

Function	Description
emalloc()	Serves as replacement for malloc().
efree()	Serves as replacement for free().
estrdup()	Serves as replacement for strdup().
estrndup()	Serves as replacement for strndup(). Faster than estrdup() and binary-safe. This is the recommended function to use if you know the string length prior to duplicating it.
ecalloc()	Serves as replacement for calloc().
erealloc()	Serves as replacement for realloc().

Table 5: Memory Management Functions

Memory allocated by the above functions is considered local to the current process and is discarded as soon as the script executed by the process is terminated.

Directory and File Functions

The following directory and file functions work exactly as their C counterparts, but they provide virtual working directory support at the thread level.

Zend Function	Regular C Function
V_GETCWD()	getcwd()
V_FOPEN()	fopen()
V_OPEN()	open()
V_CHDIR()	chdir()
V_GETWD()	getwd()
V_CHDIR_FILE()	Takes a file path as an argument and changes the current working directory to that file's directory.
V_STAT()	stat()
V_LSTAT()	lstat()

Table 6: Directory and File Functions

It is important to use these functions in your extension as to avoid worrying about the virtual working directory and its associated implied restrictions in PHP.

config.m4 and PHP's Automatic Build System

Critical to building extensions is the automatic build system, encapsulated generally in the script *configure*. When you create a new extension, you expect that its build process will be integrated into the general PHP build system. Fortunately the *ext_skel* script creates a default **config.m4** file that can be used to update the *configure* script for building PHP. PHP uses **m4**, a macro processor to facilitate the updates to its build system. For more information about **m4**, visit http://www.gnu.org/manual/m4/html_mono/m4.ht ml.

There are several general macros to be used within the context of PHP extensions that will be used. They are shown in the table below. By default, the *ext_skel* script creates a macro file that is completely commented (comments are delimited by **dnl**) and therefore affects no files when initially run.

Macro	Description
PHP_ARG_ENABLE (arg-name, check message, help text[, default-val[, extension-or-not]])	When arg-name is the name of an extension, this macro allows a configuration flag of *enable arg name*. The simple example above uses this macro in its *config.m4* file.
PHP_ARG_WITH (arg-name, check message, help text[, default-val[, extension-or-not]])	Same as above, but allows for a configuration flag of *with arg name=/path/to/source*.
AC_MSG_CHECKING (message)	Prints a "checking <message>" text during configure.
AC_MSG_RESULT (value)	Gives the result to AC_MSG_CHECKING; should specify either yes or no as value.
AC_MSG_ERROR (message)	Prints message as error message during configure and aborts the script.
AC_DEFINE (name, value, description)	Adds #define to php_config.h with the value of value and a comment that says description (this is useful for conditional compilation of your module).
AC_ADD_INCLUDE (path)	Adds a compiler include path; for example, used if the module needs to add search paths for header files.
AC_ADD_LIBRARY_WIT H_PATH (libraryname,	Specifies an additional library to link.

librarypath)	
AC_ARG_WITH (modulename, description, unconditionaltest, conditionaltest)	Quite a powerful macro, adding the module with description to the configure --help output. PHP checks whether the option --with-<modulename> is given to the configure script. If so, it runs the script unconditionaltest (for example, --with-myext=yes), in which case the value of the option is contained in the variable $withval. Otherwise, it executes conditionaltest.
PHP_NEW_EXTENSION (extname, sources [, shared [,sapi_class[, extra-cflags]]])	Preferred macro for enabling a new extension in PHP. The *extname* is the name of the extension/the subdirectory where it resides. *sources* is a list of files relative to the subdirectory that are used to build the extension. The *shared* parameter can be set to **shared** or **yes** to build the extension as a dymanically loadable library. Optional parameter *sapi_class* can be set to "cli" to mark extension build only with CLI or CGI sapi's. *extra cflags* are passed to the compiler, with @ext_srcdir@ being substituted.
PHP_EXTENSION (modulename, [shared])	You can supply a second argument in addition to your module name, indicating whether you intend compilation as a shared module. This will result in a definition at compile time for your source as COMPILE_DL_<modulename>. The above macro, PHP_NEW_EXTENSION, is preferred.
PHP_CHECK_LIBRARY(library, function [, action-found [, action-not-found [, extra-libs]]])	Checks the library file specified by *library* for the function called *function*. If the named function exists, the macros in *action found* are executed, otherwise the macros in *action not found* are executed. The *extra libs* parameter specifies additional libraries that are required to build PHP with *library*.

Table 7: Some macros available for use within the config.m4 file.

The use of the above macros may not yet be entirely clear, but the complex extension example below will help clarify these macros. It is important to identify the difference between PHP_ARG_ENABLE and PHP_ARG_WITH. From a build perspective, these macros change the parameters of the *configure* script. The first form was used in the simple example above to allow for the configure script to be executed as:

./configure --enable-first_test

Had we used the second macro, the above line would have failed and the command would have been issued as:

./configure --with-first_test=/expected/path

Typically the second form is used when PHP needs to link against an external library (.so).

> NOTE: Any time you modify the *config.m4* file, you must re-run the *buildconf* script. Additionally you may need to delete the *config.cache* file before running the *configure* script to ensure that any changes will have any effect on the build process.

Revisiting the *config.m4* file from the simple example (comments removed), it becomes clear that a very few configuration macros are actually required to create a new PHP extension. In fact, only 2 macros are required as shown below.

```
1    PHP_ARG_ENABLE(first_test, whether to enable
     first_test support,
```

```
2   [ --enable-first_test              Enable
    first_test support])

3
4   if test "$PHP_FIRST_TEST" != "no"; then
5     PHP_NEW_EXTENSION(first_test,
    first_test.c, $ext_shared)
6   fi
```

**Code Fragment 11: config.m4 from first_test project
showing only relevant lines.**

The first macro provides the facility by which the
extension can be added to the *configure* command line
and the second macro conditionally adds the
extension to the build process.

Exported Functions Delaration

When you use *ext_skel* and a prototype file to generate
the C function stubs, you will notice that all of the
exported functions created have a simple prototype
such as the following:

```
1   PHP_FUNCTION(func1)
```

For the above, the PHP_FUNCTION macro
expands to create the following C function
declaration:

```
1   void zif_func1( int ht
2                         , zval * return_value
3                         , zval * this_ptr
4                         , int return_value_used
5                         , zend_executor_globals
    * executor_globals
6                         );
```

**Code Fragment 12: C code expansion of the
PHP_FUNCTION prototype macro.**

You will notice that the actual internal function name is **zif_func1**. The parameters of the function are described below:

Parameter	Description
ht	The number of arguments passed to the Zend function. You should not touch this directly, but instead use ZEND_NUM_ARGS() to obtain the value.
return_value	This variable is used to pass any return values of your function back to PHP. Access to this variable is best done using the predefined macros. A list of these macros is available later in this document.
this_ptr	Using this variable, you can gain access to the object in which your function is contained, if it's used within an object. Use the function getThis() to obtain this pointer.
return_value_used	This flag indicates whether an eventual return value from this function will actually be used by the calling script. 0 indicates that the return value is not used; 1 indicates that the caller expects a return value. Evaluation of this flag can be done to verify correct usage of the function as well as speed optimizations in case returning a value requires expensive operations (for an example, see how array.c makes use of this).
executor_globals	This variable points to global settings of the Zend engine. You'll find this useful when creating new variables, for example (more about this later). The executor globals can also be introduced to your function by using the macro TSRMLS_FETCH().

Table 8: Parameters to a function prototyped by PHP_FUNCTION.

Much of the information in this subsection is for your information only. Most of the time, you will use macros and helper functions to access and update the above variables. However, in some instances you will access these values directly and therefore you must understand them.

Creating Constants

When creating extensions, it is possible to provide the end-programmer with new constants. Such constants may be then used as parameters to extension functions or to compare against return values. The following table shows the macros that are available:

Macro	Description
REGISTER_LONG_CONSTANT(name, value, flags) REGISTER_MAIN_LONG_CONSTANT(name, value, flags)	Registers a new constant of type long.
REGISTER_DOUBLE_CONSTANT(name, value, flags) REGISTER_MAIN_DOUBLE_CONSTANT(name, value, flags)	Registers a new constant of type double.
REGISTER_STRING_CONSTANT(name, value, flags) REGISTER_MAIN_STRING_CONSTANT(name, value, flags)	Registers a new constant of type string. The specified string must reside in Zend's internal memory.
REGISTER_STRINGL_CONSTANT(name, value, length, flags) REGISTER_MAIN_STRINGL_CONSTANT(name, value, length, flags)	Registers a new constant of type string. The string length is explicitly set to length. The specified string must reside in Zend's internal memory.

Table 9: Macros for Creating Constants

There are two types of macros – REGISTER_*_CONSTANT and REGISTER_MAIN_*_CONSTANT. The former type creates constants bound to the extension module. These constants are dumped from the symbol table as soon as the module that registered the constant is unloaded from memory. The latter type creates constants that persist in the symbol table independently of the module.

Each of the macros above accepts a name and value (and a length for the STRINGL versions) and a set of flags. The flags available for use are:

- CONST_CS – This constant's name is to be treated as case sensitive
- CONST_PERSISTENT – This constant is persistent and won't be *forgotten* when the current process carrying this constant is shut down

A simple usage example is shown below:

```
1   // register a new constant of type "long"
2   REGISTER_LONG_CONSTANT("MY_CONSTANT", 1234,
    CONST_CS |    CONST_PERSISTENT);
```

Arguments and Return Values

Overview

In the simple example the function **zend_parse_parameters** was introduced and used with little explanation. This single function is the preferred method for accessing arguments passed into your extension's functions. However, some types of arguments cannot be fully managed with this function, so more detail is provided in this subsection.

The **zend_parse_parameters** function is relatively new to PHP, introduced between PHP 4.0.6 and PHP 4.1.0. Because argument parsing is so commonly used, this function was introduced to simplify the process. The prototype of this function is:

```
1   int zend_parse_parameters(int num_args
        TSRMLS_DC, char *type_spec, ...);
```

The *num_args* parameter is the actual number of arguments passed to the extension function. Use the ZEND_NUM_ARGS macro to retrieve this value. The second parameter should always be TSRMLS_CC macro. The third argument is a string that specifies the number and types of arguments your extension function is expecting, similar to how printf format string specifies the number and format of the output values it should operate on. And finally the rest of the arguments are pointers to variables which should receive the values from the parameters.

The type specifiers are:

l	Long
d	Double
s	String
b	Boolean
r	Resource
a	Array
o	Object of any class
O	Object of class specified by the class entry
z	Actual zval

Table 10: Type specifiers for the zend_parse_parameters() function.

The following characters also have special meaning in the specifier string.

| (pipe)	Indicates that the remaining parameters are optional. The storage variables corresponding to these parameters should be initialized to default values by the extension,

	since they will not touched by the parsing function if the parameters are not passed.
/	The parsing function will call SEPARATE_ZVAL_IF_NOT_REF() on the parameter it follows which will create a copy of the parameter unless the parameter is a reference.
!	The parameter it follows can be specified type or NULL. If NULL is passed by the user, the storage pointer will be set to NULL. This only applies to arrays, objects, resources and zvals (types a, o, O, r and Z).

Table 11: Type specification modifiers for the zend_parse_parameters() function.

When using the *ext_skel* script, the generated C code will contain a reference to the **zend_parse_parameters** function for each function defined in the prototype file. The simple extension has the following code and the associated function prototypes:

```
1   // proto double calcpi(int iterations)
2       if (zend_parse_parameters(argc
    TSRMLS_CC, "l", &iterations) == FAILURE)
    return;
3
4   // proto string reverse(string input)
5       if (zend_parse_parameters(argc
    TSRMLS_CC, "s", &input, &input_len) ==
    FAILURE) return;
6
7   // proto array uniquechars(string input [,
    bool case_sensitive])
8       if (zend_parse_parameters(argc
    TSRMLS_CC, "s|b", &input, &input_len,
    &case_sensitive) == FAILURE) return;
```

Code Fragment 13: Examples of zend_parse_parameters() from the first_test sample project.

The **calcpi** function accepts a single integer parameter and therefore passes the single character **l** as its type specification string. Note that a single string value (line 5) has a single character type specifier, but requires two argument pointers to parse out the string, the first, *input* is a character pointer (char*) and the second is an integer which will contain the length of the string. The **uniquechars** function accepts two parameters, but the second parameter is optional. Note the specification string is **s | b** in line 8 above.

If you need to change the number or types of arguments to a function in your extension, but do not wish to create a new prototype or use the *ext_skel* script, you should become familiar with using the **zend_parse_parameters** function. Some additional examples from the PHP site itself are below:

```
1   /* Gets a long, a string and its length, and
    a zval. */
2   long l;
3   char *s;
4   int s_len;
5   zval *param;
6   if (zend_parse_parameters(ZEND_NUM_ARGS()
    TSRMLS_CC,
7                             "lsz", &l, &s,
    &s_len, &param) == FAILURE) {
8       return;
9   }
10
11  /* Gets an object of class specified by
    my_ce, and an optional double. */
12  zval *obj;
13  double d = 0.5;
14  if (zend_parse_parameters(ZEND_NUM_ARGS()
    TSRMLS_CC,
15                            "O|d", &obj,
    my_ce, &d) == FAILURE) {
16      return;
17  }
18
19  /* Gets an object or null, and an array.
20     If null is passed for object, obj will be
    set to NULL. */
21  zval *obj;
22  zval *arr;
23  if (zend_parse_parameters(ZEND_NUM_ARGS()
    TSRMLS_CC, "O!a", &obj, &arr) == FAILURE) {
```

```
24      return;
25  }
26
27  /* Gets a separated array. */
28  zval *arr;
29  if (zend_parse_parameters(ZEND_NUM_ARGS()
    TSRMLS_CC, "a/", &arr) == FAILURE) {
30      return;
31  }
32
33  /* Get only the first three parameters
    (useful for varargs functions). */
34  zval *z;
35  zend_bool b;
36  zval *r;
37  if (zend_parse_parameters(3, "zbr!", &z, &b,
    &r) == FAILURE) {
38      return;
39  }
```

Code Fragment 14: Additional examples of the zend_parse_parameters() function.

The last example shows how you can use the **zend_parse_parameters** function to retrieve just a partial set of the parameters. This can be useful if your PHP function accepts a variable number of arguments that follow a set of normal arguments. To obtain the arguments for a variable argument function, you will eventually need to use the **zend_get_parameters_array_ex** function. This function will be detailed later.

There may be instances where you need or want to create a function with entirely different parameters and types. This could be used to overload a function name and provide functionality for different parameter types. In order to do this, there is another function, **zend_parse_parameters_ex,** which has another parameter that currently has one used value that ensures no error messages are generated during parsing. By way of example, the following will allow the argument list to contain either two integers or a string and two doubles as its parameters.

```
1   long l1, l2;
2   char *s;
3   int s_len;
4   double d1, d2;
5
6   if
    (zend_parse_parameters_ex(ZEND_PARSE_PARAMS_
    QUIET,
7                              ZEND_NUM_ARGS()
    TSRMLS_CC,
8                                "ll", &l1, &l2)
    == SUCCESS) {
9   } else if
    (zend_parse_parameters_ex(ZEND_PARSE_PARAMS_
    QUIET,
10
    ZEND_NUM_ARGS(), "sdd", &s, &s_len,
11                                      &d1,
    &d2) == SUCCESS) {
12  } else {
13      php_error(E_WARNING, "%s() takes either
    two integers or a string and two doubles as
    its arguments",
14
    get_active_function_name(TSRMLS_C));
15      return;
16  }
```

Code Fragment 15: Using zend_parse_parameters_ex().

To implement a function that accepts a variable argument list, you must use the **zend_get_parameters_array_ex** function. This function accepts two parameters, the number of arguments to retrieve and an array in which to store them. For example, the following code can be used in a function that accepts 2, 3, 4 or 5 parameters.

```
1   zval **parameter_array[5];
2   /* get the number of arguments */
3   argument_count = ZEND_NUM_ARGS();
4
5   /* see if it satisfies our minimal request
    (2 arguments) */
6   /* and our maximal acceptance (5 arguments)
    */
7   if(argument_count < 2 || argument_count > 5)
8       WRONG_PARAM_COUNT;
```

```
9
10  /* argument count is correct, now retrieve
    arguments */
11  if(zend_get_parameters_array_ex(argument_cou
    nt, parameter_array) != SUCCESS)
12      WRONG_PARAM_COUNT;
```

Code Fragment 16: Using zend_get_parameters_array_ex().

The **WRONG_PARAM_COUNT** macro is used to print a standard error reporting that the argument count is invalid. The above example is not a great example of truly variable arguments as it assumes an upper limit, but it provides a foundation from which to build functions that have truly dynamic argument lists. One item to note is that all arguments accessed using this function are returned as the standard PHP zval type. To use variables of this type requires helper functions and macros described later.

When you create an extension function that has a argument list that isn't completely serviced by the **zend_parse_parameters** function, or if the argument type is such that you must work with the PHP zval type, it is important to understand this type and which macros and functions are available for using this type.

The zval type is defined in *Zend/zend.h* as:

```
1   typedef struct _zval_struct zval;
2   typedef struct _zend_class_entry
    zend_class_entry;
3
4   typedef struct _zend_object {
5           zend_class_entry *ce;
6           HashTable *properties;
7   } zend_object;
8
9   typedef union _zvalue_value {
10          long lval;
    /* long value */
```

```
11          double dval;
       /* double value */
12          struct {
13                  char *val;
14                  int len;
15          } str;
16          HashTable *ht;
       /* hash table value */
17          zend_object obj;
18   } zvalue_value;
19

20

21   struct _zval_struct {
22          /* Variable information */
23          zvalue_value value;                /*
       value */
24          zend_uchar type;        /* active
       type */
25          zend_uchar is_ref;
26          zend_ushort refcount;
27   };
```

Code Fragment 17: Type definition of zval.

> NOTE: For compatibility with PHP 3, the
> following typedef also exists:
>
> **typedef zval pval;**
>
> You will often see extensions use pval instead of
> zval.

As illustrated by the definition, a zval is a structure that at the most basic level contains a type value and a union structure representing the actual data stored. While it is possible to modify the type and contents of a zval directly, it is not recommended. The following functions are used to coerce a zval into a type (each function accepts a zval** argument):

Function	Description
convert_to_boolean_ex()	Forces conversion to a Boolean type. Boolean values remain untouched. Longs, doubles, and strings containing 0 as well as

	NULL values will result in Boolean 0 (FALSE). Arrays and objects are converted based on the number of entries or properties, respectively that they have. Empty arrays and objects are converted to FALSE; otherwise, to TRUE. All other values result in a Boolean 1 (TRUE).
convert_to_long_ex()	Forces conversion to a long, the default integer type. NULL values, Booleans, resources, and of course longs remain untouched. Doubles are truncated. Strings containing an integer are converted to their corresponding numeric representation, otherwise resulting in 0. Arrays and objects are converted to 0 if empty, 1 otherwise.
convert_to_double_ex()	Forces conversion to a double, the default floating-point type. NULL values, Booleans, resources, longs, and of course doubles remain untouched. Strings containing a number are converted to their corresponding numeric representation, otherwise resulting in 0.0. Arrays and objects are converted to 0.0 if empty, 1.0 otherwise.
convert_to_string_ex()	Forces conversion to a string. Strings remain untouched. NULL values are converted to an empty string. Booleans containing TRUE are converted to "1", otherwise resulting in an empty string. Longs and doubles are converted to their corresponding string representation. Arrays are converted to the string "Array" and objects to the string "Object".
convert_to_array_ex(value)	Forces conversion to an array. Arrays remain untouched. Objects are converted to an array by assigning all their properties to the array table. All property names are

	used as keys, property contents as values. NULL values are converted to an empty array. All other values are converted to an array that contains the specific source value in the element with the key 0.
convert_to_object_ex(value)	Forces conversion to an object. Objects remain untouched. NULL values are converted to an empty object. Arrays are converted to objects by introducing their keys as properties into the objects and their values as corresponding property contents in the object. All other types result in an object with the property scalar , having the corresponding source value as content.
convert_to_null_ex(value)	Forces the type to become a NULL value, meaning empty.

Table 12: zval type conversion functions.

If you are providing a function that accepts a by-reference argument and you intend to modify that value, you will need to do some additional work. First you must check that the argument was passed by reference using the **PZVAL_IS_REF** macro. If this returns true, you can then safely modify the zval. If not, you should not modify the value.

For example, the following code is a modified version of the **calcpi** function that illustrates what you *can* do, but exactly what you should not do:

```
1    /* {{{ proto double calcpi(int iterations)
2       Calculate Pi */
3    PHP_FUNCTION(calcpi)
4    {
5        int argc = ZEND_NUM_ARGS();
6        long iterations;
7        int index, hits;
8        double randx, randy, distance, value;
```

```
 9
10      zval **parameters[1];
11      zval **parameter;
12
13      if (zend_parse_parameters(argc
    TSRMLS_CC, "l", &iterations) == FAILURE)
14          return;
15
16
17      hits = 0;
18      for ( index = 0; index < iterations;
    index++ )
19      {
20          randx = rand();
21          randy = rand();
22
23          randx /= RAND_MAX;
24          randy /= RAND_MAX;
25
26          distance = sqrt( ( randx * randx ) + (
    randy * randy ) );
27
28          if ( distance <= 1.0 )
29          {
30            hits++;
31          }
32          value = ( (double) hits / (double)
    index );
33          value *= 4.0;
34      }
35
36      value  = ( (double) hits / (double)
    iterations );
37      value *= 4.0;
38      RETVAL_DOUBLE( value );
39
40      zend_get_parameters_array_ex( 1,
    parameters );
41      parameter = parameters[0];
42      convert_to_long_ex( parameter );
43      ZVAL_LONG( *parameter, 2 );
44  }
45  /* }}} */
```

**Code Fragment 18: Modified calcpi() showing bogus
argument write.**

Lines 40 through 43 are the added code. Lines 40
and 41 illustrate how to retrieve the zval version of
the arguments. Line 42 converts the first argument's

type to long and line 43 sets the value. The following test script can be used to illustrate the problem:

```
1   <?php
2       $aval = 10;
3       $ares = calcpi( $aval );
4       print( "ares = $ares, aval = $aval\n" );
5   ?>
```

Code Fragment 19: Test script using Code Fragment 18

The output of the above script is:

ares = 2.8, aval = 2

There are several problems with the implementation above. First, because Zend works internally with references, different variables may reference the same value. Write access to a zval container requires this container to contain an isolated value, meaning a value that's not referenced by any other containers. If a zval container were referenced by another container and you changed the referenced zval, you would automatically change the contents of the other container referencing this zval (because they'd simply point to the changed value and thus change their own value as well).

Second, because the parameter isn't expected to be modified by the user, the following PHP script may be written:

```
1   <?php
2       $aval = 10;
3       $ares = calcpi( 100 );
4       print( "ares = $ares, aval = $aval\n" );
5   ?>
```

Code Fragment 20: Second test script using Code Fragment 18

In this case, PHP creates an internal zval argument and loads it with the value 100 and passes that zval to the internal function. The output of running this code is:

ares = 2.88, aval = 10

While this implementation doesn't cause any fatal errors, the results are inconsistent and confusing. If you plan to modify arguments passed to a function, you must build your function to check that the arguments are passed correctly and only then should you change the arguments.

If you really need to change the argument to the **calcpi** function, this is the proper way to do it:

```
1    /* {{{ proto double calcpi(int iterations)
2       Calculate Pi */
3    PHP_FUNCTION(calcpi)
4    {
5        int argc = ZEND_NUM_ARGS();
6        long iterations;
7        int index, hits;
8        double randx, randy, distance, value;
9
10       zval **parameters[1];
11       zval **parameter;
12
13       if (zend_parse_parameters(argc
     TSRMLS_CC, "l", &iterations) == FAILURE)
14           return;
15
16
17       hits = 0;
18       for ( index = 0; index < iterations;
     index++ )
19       {
20          randx = rand();
21          randy = rand();
22
23          randx /= RAND_MAX;
24          randy /= RAND_MAX;
25
26          distance = sqrt( ( randx * randx ) + (
     randy * randy ) );
27
```

```
28          if ( distance <= 1.0 )
29          {
30             hits++;
31          }
32          value = ( (double) hits / (double)
      index );
33          value *= 4.0;
34       }
35
36       value  = ( (double) hits / (double)
      iterations );
37       value *= 4.0;
38       RETVAL_DOUBLE( value );
39
40       zend_get_parameters_array_ex( 1,
      parameters );
41       parameter = parameters[0];
42       if ( !PZVAL_IS_REF( *parameter ) )
43       {
44          zend_error( E_WARNING, "Parameter must
      be passed by reference." );
45          RETURN_NULL();
46       }
47       convert_to_long_ex( parameter );
48       ZVAL_LONG( *parameter, 2 );
49 }
50 /* }}} */
```

**Code Fragment 21: Modified calcpi() showing correct
argument write.**

Now running either of the two PHP samples above
results in the following warning message:

> **Warning: Parameter must be passed by
> reference. in /home/blake/source/php
> 4.3.2/mytest.php on line 3
> ares = , aval = 10**

The PHP example must be changed to the following
for it to work without warnings:

```
1 <?php
2    $aval = 10;
3    $ares = calcpi( &$aval );
4    print( "ares = $ares, aval = $aval\n" );
5 ?>
```

Code Fragment 22: Test PHP script showing use of Code Fragment 21

Working with Scalar Types

The simplest types of variables to use in your PHP extensions are the scalar type variables: integers, floating point numbers, strings and Booleans. As has been demonstrated above, using these types as arguments is built into the **zend_parse_parameters** functions. Additionally, if you need or choose to use the **zend_get_parameters_array** function to retrieve the arguments, you can use the following functions and macros to create a new scalar value, modify an existing scalar value or return a scalar value.

To create a new variable that you intend to either introduce into the PHP scope or use within your extension internal, use the MAKE_STD_ZVAL macro. This allocates a zval container and initializes it.

Once you have a new zval container, you can set its type and value. For scalar variables, the macros available are:

ZVAL_LONG(zval* cont, longint val)	Sets the variable, cont to the long integer value, val.
ZVAL_DOUBLE(zval* cont, double val)	Sets the variable, cont to the double value, val.
ZVAL_STRING(zval* cont, char* val, bool duplicate)	Sets the variable, cont to the string value, val. The duplicate flag indicates whether PHP should create a copy of the string using **estrdup**.

ZVAL_STRINGL(zval* cont, char* val, int, len, bool duplicate)	Sets the variable, cont to the string value, val using the string length, len. The duplicate flag indicates whether PHP should create a copy of the string using **estrdup**. This macro is much faster than the above if the length of the string is already known.
ZVAL_EMPTY_STRING(zval* cont)	Sets the variable, cont to an empty string.
ZVAL_BOOL(zval* cont, boolean val)	Sets the variable, cont to the boolean value, val.
ZVAL_TRUE(zval* cont)	Sets the variable, cont, to the boolean value TRUE.
ZVAL_FALSE(zval* cont)	Sets the variable, cont, to the boolean value FALSE.
ZVAL_NULL(zval* cont)	Sets the variable, cont, to a null value/type.

Table 13: Macros for setting zval type and value.

In order to quickly set the return value of your function to a scalar-type variable, use the following:

RETURN_LONG(longint val) RETVAL_LONG(longint val)	Returns long value, val.
RETURN_DOUBLE(double val) RETVAL_DOUBLE(double val)	Returns double value, val.
RETURN_STRING(longint val, bool duplicate) RETVAL_STRING(longint val, bool duplicate)	Returns string value, val. The duplicate flag indicates whether PHP should create a copy of the string using **estrdup**.
RETURN_STRINGL(longint val, int, len, bool duplicate) RETVAL_STRINGL(longint val, int, len, bool duplicate)	Returns string value, val using the string length, len. The duplicate flag indicates whether PHP should create a copy of the string using **estrdup**. This macro is much

	faster than the above if the length of the string is already known.
RETURN_EMPTY_STRING( ) RETVAL_EMPTY_STRING( )	Returns an empty string.
RETURN_BOOL(boolean val) RETVAL_BOOL(boolean val)	Returns the boolean value, val.
RETURN_TRUE( ) RETVAL_TRUE( )	Returns the boolean value TRUE.
RETURN_FALSE( ) RETVAL_FALSE( )	Returns the boolean value FALSE.
RETURN_NULL( ) RETVAL_NULL( )	Returns a null value/type.

Table 14: Macros to set the type and value of the return value of an extension function.

The **RETURN_XXX** macros set the return value and immediately return from the function. The **RETVAL_XXX** macros just set the return value, but do not return from the function.

If you have a zval and need to work with the value it contains, the following macros can be used to obtain the required information (all macros accept a zval as their only parameter):

Z_LVAL	Returns the long integer value of the zval.
Z_BVAL	Returns the boolean value of the zval.
Z_DVAL	Returns the double value of the zval.
Z_STRVAL	Returns the character pointer (char *) value of the zval.
Z_STRLEN	Returns the length of the string contained in the zval.
Z_ARRVAL	Returns a pointer to the internal hash table representing the array.
Z_OBJ	Returns a pointer to the object stored in the zval.
Z_OBJPROP	Returns a pointer to the internal hash table containing the array of property names for the object.

Z_OBJCE	Returns a pointer to the class entry for stored in the zval.
Z_RESVAL	Returns the resource value of the zval.

Table 15: Macros to determine the current type of a zval.

There are two other sets of macros that can be used in conjunction with the above. They are Z_xxxVAL_P and Z_xxxVAL_PP (where xxx is one of the types above). These macros accept either a zval* or a zval** parameter, respectively. For example, if you have allocated a zval* and it contains a long integer value, you can simply use:

Z_LVAL_P(var)

Rather than:

Z_LVAL(*var)

If you have a zval and need to know its current type, you can use the Z_TYPE, Z_TYPE_P or Z_TYPE_PP on a zval, zval* or zval**, respectively. The value returned will be one of: IS_NULL, IS_LONG, IS_DOUBLE, IS_STRING, IS_ARRAY, IS_OBJECT, IS_BOOL, IS_RESOURCE, IS_CONSTANT , IS_CONSTANT_ARRAY.

When you need to introduce a variable into the scope of the caller or into the global PHP scope, there are again some macros and functions that can be used to accomplish this task. The macro is **ZEND_SET_SYMBOL()** and the function is **zend_hash_update()**. The macro takes care of some additional checks and is therefore a bit slower than using just the function. The following example shows how to introduce to variables into the PHP variable space, with the first going into the local symbol table and the second into the global symbol table.

```
6    ZEND_FUNCTION(add_variables)
7    {
8        zval *new1, *new2;
9
10       MAKE_STD_ZVAL(new1);
11       MAKE_STD_ZVAL(new2);
12
13       ZVAL_LONG(new1, 100);
14       ZVAL_LONG(new2, 500);
15
16       ZEND_SET_SYMBOL(EG(active_symbol_table),
     "new_local_var", new1);
17       ZEND_SET_SYMBOL(&EG(symbol_table),
     "new_global_var", new2);
18
19       RETURN_NULL();
20
21   }
```

Code Fragment 23: Introducing variables into the PHP symbol tables.

A sample PHP script calling the above function shows usage – the output of the script is shown below that.

```
1    <?php
2      error_reporting( E_ALL );
3
4      function internal_func( )
5      {
6        print( "** Inside internal_func() **\n"
     );
7        print( "Value of new_local_var: " .
     $new_local_var . "\n" );
8        print( "Value of new_global_var: " .
     $new_global_var . "\n" );
9        add_variables ( );
10       print( "Value of new_local_var: " .
     $new_local_var . "\n" );
11       print( "Value of new_global_var: " .
     $new_global_var . "\n" );
12     }
13
14     print( "** Inside main scope **\n" );
```

```
15    print( "Value of new_local_var: " .
      $new_local_var . "\n" );
16    print( "Value of new_global_var: " .
      $new_global_var . "\n" );
17    add_variables ( );
18    print( "Value of new_local_var: " .
      $new_local_var . "\n" );
19    print( "Value of new_global_var: " .
      $new_global_var . "\n" );
20
21    internal_func();
22  ?>
```

Code Fragment 24: PHP script showing usage of Code Fragment 23.

```
1   ** Inside main scope **
2
3   Notice: Undefined variable:  new_local_var
    in /home/blake/source/php-4.3.2/mytest.php
    on line 15
4   Value of new_local_var:
5
6   Notice: Undefined variable:  new_global_var
    in /home/blake/source/php-4.3.2/mytest.php
    on line 16
7   Value of new_global_var:
8   Value of new_local_var: 100
9   Value of new_global_var: 500
10  ** Inside internal_func() **
11
12  Notice: Undefined variable:  new_local_var
    in /home/blake/source/php-4.3.2/mytest.php
    on line 7
13  Value of new_local_var:
14
15  Notice: Undefined variable:  new_global_var
    in /home/blake/source/php-4.3.2/mytest.php
    on line 8
16  Value of new_global_var:
17  Value of new_local_var: 100
18
19  Notice: Undefined variable:  new_global_var
    in /home/blake/source/php-4.3.2/mytest.php
    on line 11
20  Value of new_global_var:
```

Results/Output 3: Output of script (Code Fragment 24).

As can be seen in Results/Output 3, the local and global variable scope outside of a function are the same, so the introduction of variables into either scope makes them available (see Code Fragment 24, lines 18 and 19 and Results/Output 3, lines 8 and 9). Inside an internal script function, however, the global space is not available (unless the variable name has been identified using the **global** keyword), so the new global variable is not seen by the function (see Code Fragment 24, lines 10 and 11 and Results/Output 3, lines 17 and 19).

If you prefer to use the faster, **zend_hash_update()** function instead of the macro, the above code (Code Fragment 23) becomes:

```
1    ZEND_FUNCTION(add_variables)
2    {
3        zval *new1, *new2;
4
5        MAKE_STD_ZVAL(new1);
6        MAKE_STD_ZVAL(new2);
7
8        ZVAL_LONG(new1, 100);
9        ZVAL_LONG(new2, 500);
10
11       zend_hash_update(
12         EG(active_symbol_table),
13         "new_local_var",
14         strlen("new_local_var") + 1,
15         &new1,
16         sizeof(zval *),
17         NULL
18       );
19       zend_hash_update(
20         &EG(symbol_table),
21         "new_global_var",
22         strlen("new_global_var") + 1,
23         &new2,
24         sizeof(zval *),
25         NULL
26       );
27
28       RETURN_NULL();
29
30   }
```

Code Fragment 25: Using zend_hash_update() to update PHP symbol tables (see Code Fragment 23).

> NOTE: You may have noticed that you need to refer to **EG(symbol_table)** with an ampersand (**&**). The **active_symbol_table** variable is a pointer, but **symbol_table** is not, and both the macro and function used above require a pointer.

This subsection has introduced a large number of macros and functions that can be used to work with scalar variables and their associated zval containers. Examples and further details of their usage will be provided in the GLPK extension example later in this document.

Working with Arrays

Arrays and objects are similar in many fashions to the scalar variables discussed above. However, when setting values or retrieving values of these types, there are many more access functions and macros available. The first subsection here will discuss returning arrays or objects to the PHP caller. The next subsection will address using arrays and objects that are passed as arguments to your extension functions.

Returning array or object values is very straightforward and well documented. In fact, Code Fragment 7, the **uniquechars()** function implementation, contains some of the functions available for returning an array to the PHP caller. The set of commonly-used array functions are shown in the table below. All of the functions return **FAILURE** or **SUCCESS**.

Function	Description
add_assoc_long(zval *array, char *key, long n);	Adds an element of type long to an associative array using key,

	key.
add_assoc_unset(zval *array, char *key);	Adds an unset element to an associative array using key, **key**.
add_assoc_bool(zval *array, char *key, int b);	Adds a Boolean element to an associative array using key, **key**.
add_assoc_resource(zval *array, char *key, int r);	Adds a resource to an associative array using key, **key**.
add_assoc_double(zval *array, char *key, double d);	Adds a floating-point value to an associative array using key, **key**.
add_assoc_string(zval *array, char *key, char *str, int duplicate);	Adds a string to an associative array using key, **key**. The flag duplicate specifies whether the string contents have to be copied to Zend internal memory.
add_assoc_stringl(zval *array, char *key, char *str, uint length, int duplicate);	Adds a string with the desired length **length** to an associative array using key, **key**. Otherwise, behaves like add_assoc_string().
add_assoc_zval(zval *array, char *key, zval *value);	Adds a zval to an associative array using key, **key**. Useful for adding other arrays, objects, streams, etc...
add_index_long(zval *array, uint idx, long n);	Adds an element of type long to an indexed array using index, **idx**.
add_index_unset(zval *array, uint idx);	Adds an unset element to an indexed array using index, **idx**.
add_index_bool(zval *array, uint idx, int b);	Adds a Boolean element to an indexed array using index, **idx**.
add_index_resource(zval *array, uint idx, int r);	Adds a resource to an indexed array using index, **idx**.
add_index_double(zval *array, uint idx, double d);	Adds a floating-point value to an indexed array using index, **idx**.
add_index_string(zval *array, uint idx, char *str, int duplicate);	Adds a string to an indexed array using index, **idx**. The flag duplicate specifies whether the string contents have to be copied to Zend internal memory.
add_index_stringl(zval *array, uint idx, char *str, uint length, int duplicate);()	Adds a string with the desired length **length** to an indexed array using index, **idx**. This function is faster and binary-safe. Otherwise, behaves like add_index_string().
add_index_zval(zval *array, uint idx, zval *value);	Adds a zval to an indexed array using index, **idx**. Useful for adding other arrays, objects, streams, etc...
add_next_index_long(zval *array, long n);	Adds an element of type long to an indexed array using the next

	numeric index.
add_next_index_unset(zval *array);	Adds an unset element to an indexed array using the next numeric index.
add_next_index_bool(zval *array, int b)	Adds a Boolean element to an indexed array using the next numeric index.
add_next_index_resource(zval *array, int r)	Adds a resource to an indexed array using the next numeric index.
add_next_index_double(zval *array, double d);	Adds a floating-point value to an indexed array using the next numeric index.
add_next_index_string(zval *array, char *str, int duplicate);	Adds a string to an indexed array using the next numeric index. The flag duplicate specifies whether the string contents have to be copied to Zend internal memory.
add_next_index_stringl(zval *array, char *str, uint length, int duplicate);	Adds a string with the desired length **length** to an indexed array using the next numeric index. This function is faster and binary-safe. Otherwise, behaves like add_index_string().
add_next_index_zval(zval *array, zval *value);	Adds a zval to an indexed array using the next numeric index. Useful for adding other arrays, objects, streams, etc

Table 16: Array functions: Adding elements to an array.

The best way to describe the usage of the above functions is via example. The following code illustrates the usage of most all of the above functions.

```
1   /* {{{ proto array return_array_1()
2      Test returning array #1 */
3   PHP_FUNCTION(return_array_1)
4   {
5       if (ZEND_NUM_ARGS() != 0) {
6           WRONG_PARAM_COUNT;
7       }
8
9       array_init( return_value );
10
```

```
11        add_next_index_long( return_value, 5 );
12        add_next_index_long( return_value, 4 );
13        add_next_index_long( return_value, 3 );
14        add_next_index_long( return_value, 2 );
15        add_next_index_long( return_value, 1 );
16
17   }
18   /* }}} */
19
20   /* {{{ proto array return_array_2()
21      Test returning array #2 */
22   PHP_FUNCTION(return_array_2)
23   {
24       zval* sub_array1;
25       zval* sub_array2;
26
27       if (ZEND_NUM_ARGS() != 0) {
28           WRONG_PARAM_COUNT;
29       }
30
31       array_init( return_value );
32
33       add_next_index_long( return_value, 1 );
34       add_next_index_unset( return_value );
35       add_next_index_bool( return_value, 1 );
36       add_next_index_double( return_value,
     3.141592654 );
37       add_next_index_string( return_value,
     "Testing", 1 );
38
39       /* create a sub array to put within the
     return value */
40       MAKE_STD_ZVAL( sub_array1 );
41       array_init( sub_array1 );
42
43       add_next_index_long( sub_array1, 2 );
44       add_next_index_string( sub_array1, "This
     is the second element in the first sub-
     array", 1 );
45
46
47       /* create a sub array to put within the
     first sub array */
48       MAKE_STD_ZVAL( sub_array2 );
49       array_init( sub_array2 );
50
51       add_next_index_long( sub_array2, 2 );
52       add_next_index_string( sub_array2, "This
     is the second element in the second sub-
     array", 1 );
53
54       /* insert the sub arrays into their
     parent arrays */
55       add_next_index_zval( sub_array1,
     sub_array2 );
```

```
56      add_next_index_zval( return_value,
    sub_array1 );
57  }
58  /* }}} */
59
60  /* {{{ proto array return_array_3()
61     Test returning array #3 */
62  PHP_FUNCTION(return_array_3)
63  {
64      if (ZEND_NUM_ARGS() != 0) {
65          WRONG_PARAM_COUNT;
66      }
67
68      array_init( return_value );
69
70      add_index_long( return_value, 7, 1 );
71      add_next_index_long( return_value, 2 );
72
73      add_index_string( return_value, 300,
    "Hello, world!", 1 );
74      add_next_index_string( return_value,
    "Next index insert", 1 );
75  }
76  /* }}} */
77
78  /* {{{ proto array return_array_4()
79     Test returning array #4 */
80  PHP_FUNCTION(return_array_4)
81  {
82      if (ZEND_NUM_ARGS() != 0) {
83          WRONG_PARAM_COUNT;
84      }
85
86      array_init( return_value );
87
88      add_assoc_string( return_value, "apple",
    "red", 1 );
89      add_assoc_string( return_value,
    "banana", "yellow", 1 );
90      add_assoc_string( return_value,
    "orange", "orange", 1 );
91
92      add_assoc_long( return_value, "one", 1
    );
93      add_assoc_long( return_value, "two", 2
    );
94      add_assoc_long( return_value, "apple", 3
    );
95  }
96  /* }}} */
```

Code Fragment 26: Four examples showing how to return arrays

The first function **return_array_1**, illustrates the simplest form of an array – one that is indexed sequentially and contains homogenous data (integers in this case). The second example, **return_array_2**, continues to use a sequential index, but illustrates the method used to return heterogeneous data including sub-arrays. The third example, **return_array_3**, shows how to set specific indexes in the return array and how you can use sequential and direct indexing together. It is important to note that all arrays in PHP are internally represented as hash tables. So, while a sequentially indexed array may *feel* like a typical C array, it is not and from the PHP perspective, there is no internal difference between an array indexed by integers sequentially and an associative array. Example four, **return_array_4**, illustrates how to create an associative array. Lines 88 and 94 in Code Fragment 26 show what happens when you try to add to an array using the same index.

The following PHP script tests the above code by calling each extension function and displaying (recursively, if needed) the returned array.

```php
1   <?php
2     function dump_array( $array, $level = 0 )
3     {
4       $padding = str_repeat( ' ', $level );
5
6       foreach( $array as $key => $value )
7       {
8         print( $padding . '[' . $key . '] -> ' );
9         if ( is_array( $value ) )
10        {
11          print( "(array)\n" );
12          dump_array( $value, $level + 1 );
13        }
14        else
15        {
16          print( '(' . gettype( $value ) . ') '
        . $value . "\n" );
```

```
17          }
18      }
19    }
20
21    $array = return_array_1();
22    dump_array( $array );
23    print( "\n\n" );
24
25    $array = return_array_2();
26    dump_array( $array );
27    print( "\n\n" );
28
29    $array = return_array_3();
30    dump_array( $array );
31    print( "\n\n" );
32
33    $array = return_array_4();
34    dump_array( $array );
35    print( "\n\n" );
36  ?>
```

Code Fragment 27: PHP test for extension functions from Code Fragment 26

The output of the test script is shown below.

```
37  [0] -> (integer) 5
38  [1] -> (integer) 4
39  [2] -> (integer) 3
40  [3] -> (integer) 2
41  [4] -> (integer) 1
42
43
44  [0] -> (integer) 1
45  [1] -> (NULL)
46  [2] -> (boolean) 1
47  [3] -> (double) 3.141592654
48  [4] -> (string) Testing
49  [5] -> (array)
50    [0] -> (integer) 2
51    [1] -> (string) This is the second element
    in the first sub-array
52    [2] -> (array)
53      [0] -> (integer) 2
54      [1] -> (string) This is the second
    element in the second sub-array
55
56
57  [7] -> (integer) 1
58  [8] -> (integer) 2
59  [300] -> (string) Hello, world!
60  [301] -> (string) Next index insert
```

```
61
62
63  [apple] -> (integer) 3
64  [banana] -> (string) yellow
65  [orange] -> (string) orange
66  [one] -> (integer) 1
67  [two] -> (integer) 2
```

Results/Output 4: Ouput of PHP script (Code Fragment 27)

The same functions used in these examples can be used to create arrays to be added to the local or global scope. These are certainly the easiest and most clearly documented array manipulation functions. It is also possible to use the **zend_hash_xxx** functions to manipulate arrays. These functions are not documented on the PHP site or in any other online reference that I could find, so the following subsection of this document is based on my experience. The **zend_hash_xxx** functions are required if you expect arrays as arguments to your functions or if you need to manipulate data in any of the global hash tables, such as the PHP superglobal arrays **$_SESSION** or **$_SERVER**.

The following functions (many are actually macros that have been labeled with argument and return types) can be found in the **Zend/zend_hash.h** source file. Not all of the functions in that file are included in this table and not all are fully documented here.

int **zend_hash_update**(HashTable *ht, char *arKey, uint nKeyLength, void **pData, uint nDataSize, void **pDest)	Adds or updates a value in an associative array.
int **zend_hash_add**(HashTable *ht, char *arKey, uint nKeyLength, void **pData, uint nDataSize, void **pDest)	Adds or updates a value in an associative array.
int **zend_hash_index_update**(HashTable *ht, ulong h, void **pData, uint nDataSize, void	Adds or updates a value in an indexed

**pDest)	array.
int **zend_hash_next_index_insert**(HashTable *ht, void **pData, uint nDataSize, void **pDest)	Adds an element to a sequentially indexed array, similar to the **add_next_index_x xx** functions listed in Table 16.
int **zend_hash_del**(HashTable *ht, char *arKey, uint nKeyLength)	Deletes an element from an associative array.
int **zend_hash_index_del**(HashTable *ht, ulong h)	Deletes and element from an indexed array.
int **zend_hash_find**(HashTable *ht, char *arKey, uint nKeyLength, void **pData)	Locates the element of an associative array with key, **arKey**.
int **zend_hash_index_find**(HashTable *ht, ulong h, void **pData)	Locates the element of an indexed array with index, **h**.
int **zend_hash_move_forward**(HashTable *ht)	Moves to the next element of the array (based on an internal pointer).
int **zend_hash_move_backwards**(HashTable *ht)	Moves to the previous element of the array (based on an internal pointer).
int **zend_hash_get_current_key**(HashTable *ht, char **str_index, ulong *num_index, zend_bool duplicate)	Returns the key at the current element of the array (based on an internal pointer).
int **zend_hash_get_current_key_type**(HashTable *ht)	Returns the type of the key at the current array element (based on an internal pointer).
int **zend_hash_get_current_data**(HashTable *ht, void **pData)	Returns the data at the current array element (based on an internal pointer).
void **zend_hash_internal_pointer_reset**(HashTable *ht)	Moves the array's internal pointer to the beginning of the array.
void **zend_hash_internal_pointer_end**(HashTable	Moves the array's internal pointer to

*ht)	the end of the array.
int **zend_hash_num_elements**(HashTable *ht)	Returns the number of elements in the array.

Table 17: Array functions: Manipulating an array using the zend_hash_xxx functions.

The following example shows how to use the array traversal functions. The extension function **traverse_array** traverses forward, while **traverse_array_r** traverses the array backward. Each function accepts a single array argument and returns an array of strings (output messages).

```
1    PHP_FUNCTION(traverse_array)
2    {
3        zval*   array;
4        zval**  item;
5        int     count, i;
6        char    buffer[1024];
7
8        array_init( return_value );
9
10       if ( zend_parse_parameters(
     ZEND_NUM_ARGS() TSRMLS_CC, "a", &array ) ==
     FAILURE )
11       {
12           return;
13       }
14
15       // get number of elements in the array
16       count = zend_hash_num_elements(
     Z_ARRVAL_P( array ) );
17       sprintf( buffer, "array size = %d",
     count );
18       add_next_index_string( return_value,
     buffer, 1 );
19
20       // move to the begining of the array
21       zend_hash_internal_pointer_reset(
     Z_ARRVAL_P( array ) );
22       for ( i = 0; i < count; i ++ )
23       {
24           char* key;
25           int   ind;
26
27           // get the data in the current array
     element and coerce into a string
```

```
28          zend_hash_get_current_data(
    Z_ARRVAL_P( array ), (void**) &item );
29          convert_to_string_ex( item );
30
31          // get the key (note this function
    returns key type)
32          if ( zend_hash_get_current_key(
    Z_ARRVAL_P( array ), &key, &ind, 0 ) ==
    HASH_KEY_IS_STRING )
33          {
34              sprintf( buffer, "array[%s] = %s",
    key, Z_STRVAL_PP( item ) );
35              add_next_index_string(
    return_value, buffer, 1 );
36          }
37          else
38          {
39              sprintf( buffer, "array[%d] = %s",
    ind, Z_STRVAL_PP( item ) );
40              add_next_index_string(
    return_value, buffer, 1 );
41          }
42
43          zend_hash_move_forward( Z_ARRVAL_P(
    array ) );
44      }
45 }
46
47 PHP_FUNCTION(traverse_array_r)
48 {
49     zval*  array;
50     zval** item;
51     int    count, i;
52     char   buffer[1024];
53
54     array_init( return_value );
55
56     if ( zend_parse_parameters(
    ZEND_NUM_ARGS() TSRMLS_CC, "a", &array ) ==
    FAILURE )
57     {
58          return;
59     }
60
61     // get number of elements in the array
62     count = zend_hash_num_elements(
    Z_ARRVAL_P( array ) );
63     sprintf( buffer, "array size = %d",
    count );
64     add_next_index_string( return_value,
    buffer, 1 );
65
66     // move to the end of the array
67     zend_hash_internal_pointer_end(
    Z_ARRVAL_P( array ) );
```

```
68        for ( i = 0; i < count; i ++ )
69        {
70            char* key;
71            int   ind;
72
73            // get the data in the current array
      element and coerce into a string
74            zend_hash_get_current_data(
      Z_ARRVAL_P( array ), (void**) &item );
75            convert_to_string_ex( item );
76
77            // get the key (note this function
      returns key type)
78            if ( zend_hash_get_current_key(
      Z_ARRVAL_P( array ), &key, &ind, 0 ) ==
      HASH_KEY_IS_STRING )
79            {
80                sprintf( buffer, "array[%s] = %s",
      key, Z_STRVAL_PP( item ) );
81                add_next_index_string(
      return_value, buffer, 1 );
82            }
83            else
84            {
85                sprintf( buffer, "array[%d] = %s",
      ind, Z_STRVAL_PP( item ) );
86                add_next_index_string(
      return_value, buffer, 1 );
87            }
88
89            zend_hash_move_backwards(
      Z_ARRVAL_P( array ) );
90        }
91  }
```

Code Fragment 28: Array functions: Traversal

The first step function in each is to determine the number of items in the array (lines 16 and 62). Next the internal array pointer is set to either the beginning or end of the array, respectively (lines 21 and 67). The data for the current element is then retrieved and coerced into a string value for simplicity in this demonstration. Next the key information is retrieved (lines 32 and 78) and based on the type of the key, the appropriate information is added to the result array. Below is the source of the PHP test script used to test the array traversal functions.

```
1    <?php
2      error_reporting( E_ALL );
3      $output = traverse_array( 1 );
4      print( "Function call results:\n" .
       implode( "\n", $output ) . "\n\n" );
5
6      $output = traverse_array( array( 1, 2,
       'hello', 'apple' => 'red' ) );
7      print( "Function call results:\n" .
       implode( "\n", $output ) . "\n\n" );
8
9      $output = traverse_array_r( array( 1, 2,
       'hello', 'apple' => 'red' ) );
10     print( "Function call results
       (reverse):\n" . implode( "\n", $output ) .
       "\n\n" );
11
12     $output = traverse_array( array() );
13     print( "Function call results (empty
       array):\n" . implode( "\n", $output ) .
       "\n\n" );
14   ?>
```

Code Fragment 29: PHP script for testing Code Fragment 28, Array traversal functions

Below is the output. Note that the first call is intentionally passing an integer instead of an array to illustrate the type of general warnings that are generated by the **zend_parse_parameters** function.

```
1    Warning: traverse_array() expects parameter
     1 to be array, integer given in
     /home/blake/source/php-4.3.2/trav_test.php
     on line 3
2    Function call results:
3
4
5    Function call results:
6    array size = 4
7    array[0] = 1
8    array[1] = 2
9    array[2] = hello
10   array[apple] = red
11
12   Function call results (reverse):
13   array size = 4
14   array[apple] = red
15   array[2] = hello
```

```
16  array[1] = 2
17  array[0] = 1
18
19  Function call results (empty array):
20  array size = 0
```

Results/Output 5: Results of running PHP script (Code Fragment 29)

The next example shows how to use the array search functions to locate keys in array arguments. This is particularly useful if you are expecting an array with a specific format to be passed into your functions.

```
1   PHP_FUNCTION(array_find)
2   {
3       zval*  array;
4       zval** item;
5       int    long_index;
6       char*  string_index;
7       int    string_index_len;
8       char   buffer[1024];
9
10      array_init( return_value );
11
12      if ( zend_parse_parameters_ex(
    ZEND_PARSE_PARAMS_QUIET, ZEND_NUM_ARGS()
    TSRMLS_CC, "al", &array, &long_index ) ==
    SUCCESS )
13      {
14          // find item indexed by integer,
    long_index
15          if ( zend_hash_index_find(
    Z_ARRVAL_P( array ), long_index, (void**)
    &item ) == SUCCESS )
16          {
17              convert_to_string_ex( item );
18              sprintf( buffer, "index [%d]
    found containing data %s", long_index,
    Z_STRVAL_PP( item ) );
19              add_next_index_string(
    return_value, buffer, 1 );
20
21              zend_hash_get_current_data(
    Z_ARRVAL_P( array ), (void**) &item );
    convert_to_string_ex( item );
22              sprintf( buffer, "data at
    current array location: %s", Z_STRVAL_PP(
    item ) );
23              add_next_index_string(
    return_value, buffer, 1 );
```

```
24            }
25          else
26          {
27              sprintf( buffer, "index [%d] not
       found in array", long_index );
28              add_next_index_string(
       return_value, buffer, 1 );
29          }
30        }
31        else if ( zend_parse_parameters_ex(
       ZEND_PARSE_PARAMS_QUIET, ZEND_NUM_ARGS()
       TSRMLS_CC, "as", &array, &string_index,
       &string_index_len ) == SUCCESS )
32        {
33          // find item indexed by assoc
       string, string_index
34          if ( zend_hash_find( Z_ARRVAL_P(
       array ), string_index, string_index_len + 1,
       (void**) &item ) == SUCCESS )
35          {
36              convert_to_string_ex( item );
37              sprintf( buffer, "index ['%s']
       found containing data %s", string_index,
       Z_STRVAL_PP( item ) );
38              add_next_index_string(
       return_value, buffer, 1 );
39
40              zend_hash_get_current_data(
       Z_ARRVAL_P( array ), (void**) &item );
41              convert_to_string_ex( item );
42              sprintf( buffer, "data at
       current array location: %s", Z_STRVAL_PP(
       item ) );
43              add_next_index_string(
       return_value, buffer, 1 );
44          }
45          else
46          {
47              sprintf( buffer, "index ['%s']
       not found in array", string_index );
48              add_next_index_string(
       return_value, buffer, 1 );
49          }
50        }
51        else
52        {
53          php_error( E_WARNING, "usage %s(
       array, [string|integer] )",
       get_active_function_name( TSRMLS_C ) );
54          RETURN_FALSE;
55        }
56 }
```

Code Fragment 30: Array functions: Finding keys

The **array_find** function demonstrates methods for locating keys within an array. This function accepts an array and either a string or integer parameter. This demonstrates a practical method for using the **zend_parse_parameters_ex** function.

If the first call to **zend_parse_parameters_ex** succeeds, then the user has passed an integer key and the find function on line 15 is **zend_hash_index_find**. This function assumes that they array is indexed by integers and attempts to find the key. If the key is found, a success line is added to the result output array. Additionally, lines 21-23 are included to show that while the **zend_hash_index_find** function may find the array key, it does not update the internal array pointer to the location found. This fact is just informational.

Lines 31 to 50 perform the same actions in the case that the index being sought is a string (associative array). Note that when passing the length of the key to the **zend_hash_find** function, you must include the null terminator as part of the length (see line 34).

A sample test script is below.

```
1    <?php
2      $array1 = array( 'one', 'two', 'three',
     'four' );
3      $array2 = array( 'one' => 1, 'two' => 2,
     'three' => 3, 'four' => 4 );
4
5      $output = array_find( $array1, 3 );
6      print( implode( "\n", $output ) . "\n\n"
     );
7
8      $output = array_find( $array1, 5 );
9      print( implode( "\n", $output ) . "\n\n"
     );
10
11     $output = array_find( $array1, 'one' );
```

```
12    print( implode( "\n", $output ) . "\n\n"
      );
13
14    $output = array_find( $array2, 'two' );
15    print( implode( "\n", $output ) . "\n\n"
      );
16
17    $output = array_find( $array2, 'bogus' );
18    print( implode( "\n", $output ) . "\n\n"
      );
19
20    $output = array_find( $array2, 4 );
21    print( implode( "\n", $output ) . "\n\n"
      );
22
23    $output = array_find( 1, 2 );
24    print( implode( "\n", $output ) . "\n\n"
      );
25  ?>
```

**Code Fragment 31: PHP script to test array find functions
(Code Fragment 30)**

This example sets up two arrays. The first is indexed
by integers, the second is associative. The function
then performs searches using the **array_find** function
and reports. The output is below.

```
1   index [3] found containing data four
2   data at current array location: one
3
4   index [5] not found in array
5
6   index ['one'] not found in array
7
8   index ['two'] found containing data 2
9   data at current array location: 1
10
11  index ['bogus'] not found in array
12
13  index [4] not found in array
14
15
16  Warning: usage array_find( array,
    [string|integer] ) in
    /home/blake/source/php-4.3.2/array_find.php
    on line 23
```

**Results/Output 6: Results of the array_find() function
(Code Fragment 31)**

The results are as expected. Note that when the key is found (such as lines 1 and 2), the value returned by the find function is the expected value, but that the array's internal pointer is still pointing to the first element of the array.

Deleting elements from an array is very similar to finding elements. The following code fragment shows how to use the array delete functions. Below that is a test PHP script to exercise the functions. The implementation here is simplistic but illustrates usage. Note that the **array_delete** function relies on the array argument to be passed by reference.

```
1   PHP_FUNCTION(array_delete)
2   {
3       zval*   array;
4       zval**  item;
5       int     long_index;
6       char*   string_index;
7       int     string_index_len;
8       char    buffer[1024];
9
10      array_init( return_value );
11
12      if ( zend_parse_parameters_ex(
    ZEND_PARSE_PARAMS_QUIET, ZEND_NUM_ARGS()
    TSRMLS_CC, "al", &array, &long_index ) ==
    SUCCESS )
13      {
14          if ( !PZVAL_IS_REF( array ) )
15          {
16              php_error( E_WARNING, "The array
    parameter must be passed by reference" );
17              return;
18          }
19
20          // delete item indexed by integer,
    long_index
21          zend_hash_index_del( Z_ARRVAL_P(
    array ), long_index );
22      }
23      else if ( zend_parse_parameters_ex(
    ZEND_PARSE_PARAMS_QUIET, ZEND_NUM_ARGS()
    TSRMLS_CC, "as", &array, &string_index,
    &string_index_len ) == SUCCESS )
24      {
```

```
25          if ( !PZVAL_IS_REF( array ) )
26          {
27              php_error( E_WARNING, "The array
        parameter must be passed by reference" );
28              return;
29          }
30
31          // delete item indexed by assoc
        string, string_index
32              zend_hash_del( Z_ARRVAL_P( array ),
        string_index, string_index_len + 1 );
33          }
34      else
35      {
36          php_error( E_WARNING, "usage %s(
        &array, [string|integer] )",
        get_active_function_name( TSRMLS_C ) );
37          RETURN_FALSE;
38      }
39  }
```

Code Fragment 32: Array functions: Deleting elements

```
1   <?php
2     function dump_array( $array, $level = 0 )
3     {
4       $padding = str_repeat( ' ', $level );
5
6       foreach( $array as $key => $value )
7       {
8         print( $padding . '[' . $key . '] -> '
    );
9         if ( is_array( $value ) )
10        {
11          print( "(array)\n" );
12          dump_array( $value, $level + 1 );
13        }
14        else
15        {
16          print( '(' . gettype( $value ) . ')'
    ' . $value . "\n" );
17        }
18      }
19    }
20
21    $array1 = array( 'one', 'two', 'three',
    'four' );
22    $array2 = array( 'one' => 1, 'two' => 2,
    'three' => 3, 'four' => 4 );
23
24    array_delete( &$array1, 'one' );
25    dump_array( $array1 ); print( "\n\n" );
26    array_delete( &$array1, 1 );
27    dump_array( $array1 ); print( "\n\n" );
28
```

```
29    array_delete( &$array2, 'one' );
30    dump_array( $array2 ); print( "\n\n" );
31    array_delete( &$array2, 1 );
32    dump_array( $array2 ); print( "\n\n" );
33  ?>
```

Code Fragment 33: Using the array_delete() function (see Code Fragment 32)

The output from the above script is shown below. Again, the output is exactly as expected.

```
1    [0] -> (string) one
2    [1] -> (string) two
3    [2] -> (string) three
4    [3] -> (string) four
5
6
7    [0] -> (string) one
8    [2] -> (string) three
9    [3] -> (string) four
10
11
12   [two] -> (integer) 2
13   [three] -> (integer) 3
14   [four] -> (integer) 4
15
16
17   [two] -> (integer) 2
18   [three] -> (integer) 3
19   [four] -> (integer) 4
```

Results/Output 7: Output from running array_delete() test (Code Fragment 33)

Working with Objects

The mechanisms for working with objects are similar or the same as working with arrays. In fact, objects are also represented internally as hash tables, so the functions listed in the preceding section apply equally to objects. One area of object manipulation that differs from array manipulation is the set of helper functions available to add properties to an object. These functions are listed in the following table.

Function	Description
add_property_long(zval *object, char *key, long l);	Adds a long to the object.
add_property_unset(zval *object, char *key);	Adds an unset property to the object.
add_property_bool(zval *object, char *key, int b);	Adds a Boolean to the object.
add_property_resource(zval *object, char *key, long r);	Adds a resource to the object.
add_property_double(zval *object, char *key, double d);	Adds a double to the object.
add_property_string(zval *object, char *key, char *str, int duplicate);	Adds a string to the object.
add_property_stringl(zval *object, char *key, char *str, uint length, int duplicate);	Adds a string of the specified length to the object. This function is faster than add_property_string and also binary-safe.
add_property_zval(zval *obect, char *key, zval *container):	Adds a zval container to the object. This is useful if you have to add properties which aren't simple types like integers or strings but arrays or other objects.

Table 18: Object functions: Adding properties

An example of how to create, initialize and set values to an object is shown below. This example assumes that the returned object is more like a C structure than a true PHP object since the object contains no code. A detailed example showing how to introduce true PHP objects is discussed later.

```
1   PHP_FUNCTION( return_object )
2   {
3     zval* array;
4     zval* emb_obj;
5
6     object_init( return_value );
7
```

```
 8      add_property_long( return_value,
    "long_property", 1 );
 9      add_property_unset( return_value,
    "unset_property" );
10      add_property_bool( return_value,
    "bool_property", 1 );
11      add_property_double( return_value,
    "double_property", 3.1415926 );
12      add_property_string( return_value,
    "string_property", "This is a string", 1 );
13
14      MAKE_STD_ZVAL( emb_obj );
15      object_init( emb_obj );
16
17      add_property_long( emb_obj,
    "long_property", 2 );
18      add_property_unset( emb_obj,
    "unset_property" );
19      add_property_bool( emb_obj,
    "bool_property", 0 );
20      add_property_double( emb_obj,
    "double_property", 2.7182818 );
21      add_property_string( emb_obj,
    "string_property", "This is a string in an
    embedded sub-object", 1 );
22
23      add_property_zval( return_value,
    "object_property", emb_obj );
24
25      MAKE_STD_ZVAL( array );
26      array_init( array );
27
28      add_next_index_long( array, 1 );
29      add_next_index_long( array, 3 );
30      add_next_index_long( array, 5 );
31
32      add_property_zval( return_value,
    "array_property", array );
33  }
```

Code Fragment 34: Returning an object

The code initializes the return value to the object
type, then adds five scalar properties (lines 8 through
12). Next, simply for illustration, a second object is
created and added to the first (lines 14 through 23).
Finally, again for illustration, an array is created and
added to the object (lines 25 through 32). This simple
example is used as a basis to show how an object (or
array likewise) can contain other objects and arrays.

It becomes possible to create arrays of objects containing arrays and the like – simply by extending the examples in this document.

A PHP script to illustrate the above is below.

```
1   <?php
2     $obj = return_object();
3     var_dump( $obj );
4
5
6     print( 'double_property: ' .
    $obj->double_property . "\n" );
7     print( 'array_property[1]: ' .
    $obj->array_property[1] . "\n" );
8     print( 'object_property-
    >string_property: ' . $obj-
    >object_property->string_property .
    "\n" );
9   ?>
```

Code Fragment 35: PHP script illustrating the usage of Code Fragment 34.

The output of the above PHP script is shown below and is exactly as expected.

```
1   object(stdClass)(7) {
2     ["long_property"]=>
3     int(1)
4     ["unset_property"]=>
5     NULL
6     ["bool_property"]=>
7     bool(true)
8     ["double_property"]=>
9     float(3.1415926)
10    ["string_property"]=>
11    string(16) "This is a string"
12    ["object_property"]=>
13    object(stdClass)(5) {
14      ["long_property"]=>
15      int(2)
16      ["unset_property"]=>
17      NULL
18      ["bool_property"]=>
```

```
19       bool(false)
20       ["double_property"]=>
21       float(2.7182818)
22       ["string_property"]=>
23       string(42) "This is a string in an
      embedded sub-object"
24     }
25     ["array_property"]=>
26     array(3) {
27       [0]=>
28       int(1)
29       [1]=>
30       int(3)
31       [2]=>
32       int(5)
33     }
34  }
35  double_property: 3.1415926
36  array_property[1]: 3
37  object_property->string_property: This is a
      string in an embedded sub-object
```

Results/Output 8: Output of Code Fragment 35

To illustrate just how closely objects and arrays are
related, the following code is simply a modified
version of **traverse_array** (see Code Fragment 28)
called **traverse_object**. The properties of an object
can be thought of as an associative array.

```
1   PHP_FUNCTION(traverse_object)
2   {
3       zval*  object;
4       zval** item;
5       int    count, i;
6       char   buffer[1024];
7
8       array_init( return_value );
9
10      if ( zend_parse_parameters(
    ZEND_NUM_ARGS() TSRMLS_CC, "o", &object ) ==
    FAILURE )
11      {
12          //add_next_index_unset( return_value
    );
13          return;
14      }
15
16      // get number of elements in the object
```

```
17      count = zend_hash_num_elements(
Z_OBJPROP_P( object ) );
18      sprintf( buffer, "object property count
= %d", count );
19      add_next_index_string( return_value,
buffer, 1 );
20
21      // move to the begining of the object
properties
22      zend_hash_internal_pointer_reset(
Z_OBJPROP_P( object ) );
23      for ( i = 0; i < count; i ++ )
24      {
25          char* key;
26          int   ind;
27
28          // get the data in the current
property and coerce into a string
29          zend_hash_get_current_data(
Z_OBJPROP_P( object ), (void**) &item );
30          convert_to_string_ex( item );
31
32          // get the key (note this function
returns key type)
33          if ( zend_hash_get_current_key(
Z_OBJPROP_P( object ), &key, &ind, 0 ) ==
HASH_KEY_IS_STRING )
34          {
35              sprintf( buffer, "object->%s =
%s", key, Z_STRVAL_PP( item ) );
36              add_next_index_string(
return_value, buffer, 1 );
37          }
38          else
39          {
40              sprintf( buffer, "object->%d =
%s", ind, Z_STRVAL_PP( item ) );
41              add_next_index_string(
return_value, buffer, 1 );
42          }
43
44          zend_hash_move_forward( Z_OBJPROP_P(
object ) );
45      }
46  }
```

Code Fragment 36: Object functions: Traversal (for example only)

The only differences between the **traverse_array** function and the **traverse_object** functions are the type specifier to the **zend_parse_parameters**

function (line 10) and the general replacement of the **Z_ARRVAL_P** macro with the **Z_OBJPROP_P** macro. Otherwise there are no differences in the code.

A test script and its output are shown below.

```php
1   <?php
2     class TestObject
3     {
4       var $propOne;
5       var $propTwo;
6       var $propThree;
7       var $propFour;
8     }
9
10    $obj = new TestObject();
11    $obj->propOne = "String in propOne";
12    $obj->propTwo = 1234;
13    $obj->propThree = 3.1415926;
14    $obj->propFour  = array( 1, 2, 3, 4 );
15
16    $output = traverse_object( $obj );
17    print( implode( "\n", $output ) . "\n\n"
    );
18  ?>
```

Code Fragment 37: PHP script for testing object property traversal (Code Fragment 36)

```
1   object property count = 4
2   object->propOne = String in propOne
3   object->propTwo = 1234
4   object->propThree = 3.1415926
5   object->propFour = Array
```

Results/Output 9: Output of object property traversal (Code Fragment 37)

It should be obvious that since an object's properties are simply a hash table with string keys that updating, finding and deleting properties from an object can be accomplished using the hash functions described in the previous section. Rather than elaborating again all of the functions above, the following examples quickly illustrate the main points.

```
1   PHP_FUNCTION(obj_prop_find)
2   {
3       zval*  object;
4       zval** item;
5       char*  string_index;
6       int    string_index_len;
7       char   buffer[1024];
8
9       array_init( return_value );
10
11      if ( zend_parse_parameters(
    ZEND_NUM_ARGS() TSRMLS_CC, "os", &object,
    &string_index, &string_index_len ) !=
    SUCCESS )
12      {
13          return;
14      }
15
16      // find property with name =
    string_index
17      if ( zend_hash_find( Z_OBJPROP_P( object
    ), string_index, string_index_len + 1,
    (void**) &item ) == SUCCESS )
18      {
19          convert_to_string_ex( item );
20          sprintf( buffer, "object->%s found
    containing data %s", string_index,
    Z_STRVAL_PP( item ) );
21          add_next_index_string( return_value,
    buffer, 1 );
22      }
23      else
24      {
25          sprintf( buffer, "object->%s not
    found", string_index );
26          add_next_index_string( return_value,
    buffer, 1 );
27      }
28  }
29
30  PHP_FUNCTION(obj_prop_delete)
31  {
32      zval*  object;
33      zval** item;
34      char*  string_index;
35      int    string_index_len;
36      char   buffer[1024];
37
38      array_init( return_value );
39
```

```
40      if ( zend_parse_parameters(
    ZEND_NUM_ARGS() TSRMLS_CC, "os", &object,
    &string_index, &string_index_len ) !=
    SUCCESS )
41      {
42          return;
43      }
44
45      if ( !PZVAL_IS_REF( object ) )
46      {
47          php_error( E_WARNING, "The object
    parameter must be passed by reference" );
48          return;
49      }
50
51      // delete property with name =
    string_index
52      zend_hash_del( Z_OBJPROP_P( object ),
    string_index, string_index_len + 1 );
53  }
```

Code Fragment 38: Object functions: Finding, deleting properties

Again, the above functions are the bare bones implementations to illustrate the concepts. Very little error checking is done and the output is simple. A test PHP script and its output follow.

```
1   <?php
2       class TestObject
3       {
4           var $propOne;
5           var $propTwo;
6           var $propThree;
7           var $propFour;
8       }
9
10      $obj = new TestObject();
11      $obj->propOne = "String in propOne";
12      $obj->propTwo = 1234;
13      $obj->propThree = 3.1415926;
14      $obj->propFour = array( 1, 2, 3, 4 );
15
16      print( "Attempting to find property
    'propThree' in object:\n" );
17      $output = obj_prop_find( $obj, 'propThree'
    );
18      print( implode( "\n", $output ) . "\n\n"
    );
19
```

```
20    print( "Attempting to find property
      'propBogus' in object:\n" );
21    $output = obj_prop_find( $obj, 'propBogus'
      );
22    print( implode( "\n", $output ) . "\n\n"
      );
23
24    var_dump( $obj );
25    print( "Attempting to delete property
      'propThree' from object:\n" );
26    obj_prop_delete( &$obj, 'propThree' );
27    var_dump( $obj );
28    print( "\n\n" );
29
30  ?>
```

Code Fragment 39: PHP script to test finding, deleting object properties (Code Fragment 38)

```
1   Attempting to find property 'propThree' in
    object:
2   object->propThree found containing data
    3.1415926
3
4   Attempting to find property 'propBogus' in
    object:
5   object->propBogus not found
6
7   object(testobject)(4) {
8     ["propOne"]=>
9     string(17) "String in propOne"
10    ["propTwo"]=>
11    int(1234)
12    ["propThree"]=>
13    string(9) "3.1415926"
14    ["propFour"]=>
15    array(4) {
16      [0]=>
17      int(1)
18      [1]=>
19      int(2)
20      [2]=>
21      int(3)
22      [3]=>
23      int(4)
24    }
25  }
26  Attempting to delete property 'propThree'
    from object:
27  object(testobject)(3) {
28    ["propOne"]=>
29    string(17) "String in propOne"
30    ["propTwo"]=>
```

```
31    int(1234)
32    ["propFour"]=>
33    array(4) {
34       [0]=>
35       int(1)
36       [1]=>
37       int(2)
38       [2]=>
39       int(3)
40       [3]=>
41       int(4)
42    }
43  }
```

Results/Output 10: Output of PHP script finding, deleting object properties (Code Fragment 39)

Working with Resources

Resources are a special kind of data type in PHP. A resource doesn't refer to any specific type of data, but is an abstract method of maintaining any kind of information. For example, within the standard PHP extensions, resources are used as abstractions for file descriptors, database connections, etc. All resources are stored in resource lists internally in PHP. These lists maintain an identifier for each resource and its corresponding type definition. The Zend engine then manages all references to each resource and when the reference count reaches zero, Zend automatically calls a shutdown function for the resource.

To create a new resource, you must register a resource destruction handler. This is the handler function that will be called whenever a resource needs to be freed. When registering a destruction handler, Zend returns a *resource type handle* for the new resource. This handle is used to access the resource later. The function used to register a resource destruction handler is:

```
1  int
   zend_register_list_destructors_ex(rsrc_dtor_
   func_t ld, rsrc_dtor_func_t pld, char
   *type_name, int module_number)
```

There are two different kinds of resource destruction handlers you can pass to this function: a handler for normal resources and a handler for persistent resources. Persistent resources are for example used for database connection. When registering a resource, either of these handlers must be given; the other handler can simply be NULL.

The arguments to the **zend_register_list_destructors_ex()** function are described in the table below. The return value, again, is a unique integer ID for the new resource type.

ld	Normal resource destruction handler callback
pld	Pesistent resource destruction handler callback
type_name	A string specifying the name of your resource. It's always a good thing to specify an unique name within PHP for the resource type so when the user for example calls var_dump($resource); he also gets the name of the resource.
module_number	The module_number is automatically available in your PHP_MINIT_FUNCTION function and therefore you just pass it over.

Table 19: Arguments to the zend_register_list_destructors_ex() function.

The resource destruction handler, whether for a normal or a persistent resource, has the following prototype:

```
1  void
   resource_destruction_handler(zend_rsrc_list_
   entry *rsrc TSRMLS_DC)
```

The **rsrc** argument passed to the handler function has the following structure. The member **void *ptr** in the structure is the actual pointer to the resource you registered.

```
1   typedef struct _zend_rsrc_list_entry {
2           void *ptr;
3           int type;
4           int refcount;
5   } zend_rsrc_list_entry;
```

To use a resource passed into an extension function, the **ZEND_FETCH_RESOURCE** macro is available.

```
1   ZEND_FETCH_RESOURCE(rsrc, rsrc_type,
    rsrc_id, default_rsrc_id,
    resource_type_name, resource_type)
```

The arguments to the **ZEND_FETCH_RESOURCE** macro are shown in the table below.

rsrc	This is your pointer which will point to your previously registered resource.
rsrc_type	This is the typecast argument for your pointer, e.g. myresource *.
rsrc_id	This is the address of the zval *container the user passed to your function, e.g. &z_resource if zval *z_resource is given.
default_rsrc_id	This integer specifies the default resource ID if no resource could be fetched or -1.
resource_type_name	This is the name of the requested resource. It's a string and is used when the resource can't be found or is invalid to form a meaningful error message.
resource_type	The resource_type you got back when registering the resource destruction handler. In our example this was le_myresource.

Table 20: Arguments to the ZEND_FETCH_RESOURCE macro.

The following example illustrates the basic concepts of using resources within your extension. First the relevant changes to the header file (.h) are shown. Following that, the source code modifications are shown. Note that the *ext_skel* script automatically creates a **static int** variable for use as the resource type handle.

```
1   void general_destruction_handler(
    zend_rsrc_list_entry *rsrc TSRMLS_DC );
2
3   typedef struct _general_resource
4   {
5     FILE* fp;
6   } general_resource;
7
8   #define le_general_name "General Resource"
```

Code Fragment 40: Changes to the header (.h) file for resource handling.

```
1   /* True global resources - no need for
    thread safety here */
2   static int le_general;
3
4   ...
5
6   /* {{{ PHP_MINIT_FUNCTION
7    */
8   PHP_MINIT_FUNCTION(general)
9   {
10      zend_printf( "In PHP_MINIT_FUNCTION\n"
    );
11      ZEND_INIT_MODULE_GLOBALS(general,
    php_general_init_globals, NULL);
12      zend_printf( "global_value = %d\n",
    GENERAL_G( global_value ) );
13      REGISTER_INI_ENTRIES();
14      zend_printf( "global_value = %d\n",
    GENERAL_G( global_value ) );
15
16      le_general =
    zend_register_list_destructors_ex(
    general_destruction_handler, NULL,
    le_general_name, module_number );
17
18      return SUCCESS;
19  }
```

```
20   /* }}} */
21
22   ...
23
24   void general_destruction_handler(
     zend_rsrc_list_entry *rsrc TSRMLS_DC )
25   {
26       general_resource* resource;
27
28       zend_printf( "In
     general_destruction_handler\n" );
29
30       resource = (general_resource*) rsrc-
     >ptr;
31       fclose( resource->fp );
32       efree( resource );
33   }
34
35   PHP_FUNCTION(open_resource)
36   {
37     general_resource* resource;
38     int              rscid;
39
40     // this function accepts no arguments and
     returns a resource
41
42     resource = emalloc( sizeof(
     general_resource ) );
43     resource->fp = fopen( "/etc/hosts", "r" );
44
45     rscid = ZEND_REGISTER_RESOURCE(
     return_value, resource, le_general );
46     RETVAL_RESOURCE( rscid );
47   }
48
49   PHP_FUNCTION(read_resource)
50   {
51     general_resource* resource;
52     zval*            arg1;
53     char             fileline[1024];
54
55     // this function accepts a resource and
     returns a single line from the file
56     // abstracted by the resource
57
58     if ( zend_parse_parameters(
     ZEND_NUM_ARGS() TSRMLS_CC, "r", &arg1 ) ==
     FAILURE )
59         return;
60
61     ZEND_FETCH_RESOURCE( resource,
     general_resource *, &arg1, -1,
     le_general_name, le_general );
62
63     if ( resource )
```

```
64    {
65       if ( fgets( fileline, 1024, resource->fp
      ) )
66       {
67          RETURN_STRING( fileline, 1 );
68       }
69       else
70       {
71          RETURN_FALSE;
72       }
73    }
74  }
75
76  PHP_FUNCTION(close_resource)
77  {
78    zval*              arg1;
79
80    if ( zend_parse_parameters(
      ZEND_NUM_ARGS() TSRMLS_CC, "z", &arg1 ) ==
      FAILURE )
81       return;
82
83    zend_list_delete( Z_RESVAL_P( arg1 ) );
84  }
```

Code Fragment 41: Implementation of resource handling.

The example above is a simplistic example that opens the */etc/hosts* file and stores its file handle in the resource structure. This is not a great example since its security implications are obvious, but it is still just an example.

The changes to the header file are the declaration of the resource destruction handler (line 1), the definition of a resource structure (lines 3 through 6) and the definition of a resource name. The resource name should be unique and will appear in PHP output and error messages related to the resource.

The implementation of the resource handling includes the registration of the resource using **zend_register_list_destructors_ex** on line 16 of Code Fragment 41. The resource type handle is declared globally on line 2. Since the resource structure defined for this example contains a file handle, the resource destructor implementation (lines 24 through 33) simply closes the file and frees the resource structure. In many cases, resources will contain allocated memory and other types of system resources that will also need to be freed.

Three functions are exposed to the user, **open_resource, close_resource** and **read_resource**. The **open_resource** function (lines 35 through 47) illustrates how to allocate the new resource, register it with the Zend engine and return it to the user. The **read_resource** function illustrates how to use a resource argument passed back from the user. This is accomplished using **zend_parse_parameters** and **ZEND_FETCH_RESOURCE** together. Finally, the **close_resource** function illustrates how to remove a resource from the internal resource list using **zend_list_delete()**. It is interesting to note that the destructor function is called whether a resource is manually deleted (as in this case) or automatically deleted by the Zend engine when the reference count of the resource variable reaches zero (such as when a variable goes out of scope).

A sample PHP script showing usage is below. The output of the script also follows.

```
1    <?php
2      $res = open_resource();
3      var_dump( $res );
4
5      while( $line = read_resource( $res ) )
6        print( "line: $line\n" );
7
8      close_resource( $res );
9
10     $res1 = open_resource();
11     $res2 = open_resource();
12
```

```
13    $line1 = read_resource( $res1 );
14    print( "line 1 from resource 1: $line1\n"
      );
15    $line2 = read_resource( $res2 );
16    print( "line 2 from resource 2: $line2\n"
      );
17  ?>
```

Code Fragment 42: PHP script illustrating resource type handling.

```
1    resource(4) of type (General Resource)
2    line: 127.0.0.1 localhost.localdomain
     localhost
3
4    line: 207.44.234.60 srv01.ezmarketeers.com
     srv01
5
6    In general_destruction_handler
7    line 1 from resource 1: 127.0.0.1
     localhost.localdomain localhost
8
9    line 2 from resource 2: 127.0.0.1
     localhost.localdomain localhost
10
11   In PHP_RSHUTDOWN_FUNCTION
12   In general_destruction_handler
13   In general_destruction_handler
```

Results/Output 11: Ouput of resource script (Code Fragment 42).

Line 1 of the output is the result of the **var_dump()** call in line 3 of the script. This shows how the resource name registered in the module is used by PHP. Lines 2 and 4 are the output of the loop (lines 5 and 6 of the script). Line 6 is the output generated in the internal resource destructor function when the resource is closed on line 8 of the script. Lines 7 and 9 show that each instance of a resource is independent of any other. Lines 12 and 13 show that the resource variables are destroyed (hence the file handles are closed) when the resource variables go out of scope.

NOTE: The ZEND_FETCH_RESOURCE macro definition is:

```
#define ZEND_FETCH_RESOURCE(rsrc,
rsrc_type, passed_id, default_id,
resource_type_name, resource_type) \
        rsrc = (rsrc_type)
zend_fetch_resource(passed_id
TSRMLS_CC, default_id,
resource_type_name, NULL, 1,
resource_type);        \
        ZEND_VERIFY_RESOURCE(rsrc);
```

Where ZEND_VERIFY_RESOURCE is defined as:

```
#define ZEND_VERIFY_RESOURCE(rsrc)
\
        if (!rsrc) {
\
                RETURN_NULL();
\
        }
```

In order for the RETURN_NULL macro to work correctly, it must be used in the context of a function prototyped by PHP_FUNCTION – it must have a 'return_value' variable. If you plan to use resources from internal functions, you'll need to call the **zend_fetch_resource()** function directly. A usage example and more discussing is provided in the GLPK extension illustrated later in this document.

Duplicating Variable Contents

Eventually within a custom module you will need to copy the contents of one zval to another. Zend provides a mechanism for properly copying zval variables in the **zval_copy_ctor()** function. It is important to use this function to ensure that the zval is properly copied. This function works the same whether the zval contains a scalar value or a complex value such as an array, object or resource. The use of this function is shown in a simple example below:

```
1   zval *parameter;
2
3   if ( zend_parse_parameters( ZEND_NUM_ARGS()
    TSRMLS_CC, "z", &parameter ) == FAILURE )
4     return;
5
6   // do modifications to the parameter here
7
8   // now we want to return the modified
    container:
9   *return_value = *parameter;
10  zval_copy_ctor( return_value );
```

Code Fragment 43: Using the Zend copy constructor, zval_copy_ctor.

Assuming this code were in the context of an extension function, this example simply retrieves a single zval argument in line 3, then assigns it to the return value in line 9. If the copy constructor were not called (as in line 10), the return value would be an illegal reference to the zval passed into the function. Any changes made to either zval would be reflected in both and Zend's reference counting is rendered ineffective for this zval. To separate the return value, the copy constructor is called to duplicate the value of the argument passed.

The counterpart function, **zval_dtor()**, is the zval destructor and is described and illustrated later.

Printing Information

The **zend_printf()** function is available to introduce output to the Zend output stream. It is syntactically equivalent to the C **printf()** function. While this function may be useful during debugging, it is unlikely that your extension will normally print directly to the Zend output stream.

The **zend_error()** function is used to generate error messages. It accepts two arguments, the error type and the message itself. The error types are show below.

Error	Description
E_ERROR	Signals an error and terminates execution of the script immediately.
E_WARNING	Signals a generic warning. Execution continues.
E_PARSE	Signals a parser error. Execution continues.
E_NOTICE	Signals a notice. Execution continues. Note that by default the display of this type of error messages is turned off in php.ini.
E_CORE_ERROR	Internal error by the core; shouldn't be used by user-written modules.
E_COMPILE_ERROR	Internal error by the compiler; shouldn't be used by user-written modules.
E_COMPILE_WARNING	Internal warning by the compiler; shouldn't be used by user-written modules.

Table 21: Error codes for use with zend_error() function.

> NOTE: The **php_error()** function is another name for the **zend_error()** function. You will see **php_error()** used frequently in extensions.

If you need to include information about your extension in the output of the **phpinfo()** function, there are several functions available. PHP automatically prints a section in **phpinfo()** if you specify the ZEND_MINFO function. The *ext_skel* script creates this function and a set of default entries. The automatically generated code for the simple extension from the first part of this document is shown below.

```
1   /* {{{ PHP_MINFO_FUNCTION
2    */
3   PHP_MINFO_FUNCTION(first_test)
4   {
5       php_info_print_table_start();
6       php_info_print_table_header(2,
    "first_test support", "enabled");
7       php_info_print_table_end();
8
9       /* Remove comments if you have entries
    in php.ini
10      DISPLAY_INI_ENTRIES();
11       */
12  }
13  /* }}} */
```

Code Fragment 44: Zend MINFO_FUNCTION example.

This example illustrates the use of three of the four functions used to add content to the **php_info()** output. The functions are **php_info_print_table_start()**, **php_info_print_table_end()** (both of which take no arguments) and **php_info_print_table_header()** and **php_info_print_table_row()**. The latter two functions accept a variable argument list. The first argument is the number of columns (integers) and the subsequent arguments are the contents of each column (strings), respectively.

The last set of general print functions for use with your extensions are the **get_active_function_name()**, **zend_get_executed_filename()** and **zend_get_executed_lineno()** functions. Each of these functions receives the TSRMLS_C macro as its

only argument. The following examples illustrate
usage and output.

```
1    PHP_FUNCTION(execution_info)
2    {
3      char* temp;
4      uint  tempi;
5
6      array_init( return_value );
7
8      if ( temp = get_active_function_name(
     TSRMLS_C ) )
9          add_assoc_string( return_value,
     "function", temp, 1 );
10     else
11         add_assoc_string( return_value,
     "function", "<no function>", 1 );
12
13     if ( temp = zend_get_executed_filename(
     TSRMLS_C ) )
14         add_assoc_string( return_value, "file",
     temp, 1 );
15     else
16         add_assoc_string( return_value, "file",
     "<unknown file>", 1 );
17
18     if ( tempi = zend_get_executed_lineno(
     TSRMLS_C ) )
19         add_assoc_long( return_value, "lineno",
     tempi );
20     else
21         add_assoc_string( return_value,
     "lineno", "<unknown line>", 1 );
22
23     return;
24   }
```

Code Fragment 45: Execution Info C example

The above example simply calls each of the
aforementioned execution information functions and
assigns its return value to an associative array. Note
that the return type is either a character pointer (char
*) or integer.

```
1    <?php
2      function dump_array( $array, $level = 0 )
3      {
4          $padding = str_repeat( ' ', $level );
```

```
5
6        foreach( $array as $key => $value )
7        {
8          print( $padding . '[' . $key . '] -> '
);
9          if ( is_array( $value ) )
10         {
11           print( "(array)\n" );
12           dump_array( $value, $level + 1 );
13         }
14         else
15         {
16           print( '(' . gettype( $value ) . ')'
' . $value . "\n" );
17         }
18       }
19     }
20
21     function PrintInfo()
22     {
23       $info = execution_info();
24       dump_array( $info );
25     }
26
27     $info = execution_info();
28     dump_array( $info );
29
30     PrintInfo();
31   ?>
```

Code Fragment 46: Execution Info PHP example

The PHP example above calls the **execution_info()**
function and displays the result array. It also
illustrates what information is available contextually –
note that the current function information is the same
for both calls in the results below.

```
1    [function] -> (string) execution_info
2    [file] -> (string) /home/blake/source/php-
     4.3.2/exec_info.php
3    [lineno] -> (integer) 27
4    [function] -> (string) execution_info
5    [file] -> (string) /home/blake/source/php-
     4.3.2/exec_info.php
6    [lineno] -> (integer) 23
```

**Results/Output 12: Results of the Execution Info PHP
script**

More examples of printing information, especially as it relates to the **php_info()** function will be demonstrated later in the GLPK extension example.

Startup and Shutdown Functions

Startup and shutdown functions are available for one-time initialization and de-initialization of extension modules. The module-level startup and shutdown occur whenever a module is loaded or unloaded. For a statically linked module, this will be whenever the PHP library is loaded by the web server.

There are also request-level startup and shutdown functions. These are called at the beginning and end of each script.

For dynamically loaded modules and for cgi-based implementations all of the module and request startup will occur at the same time; similarly with the shutdown events.

The *ext_skel* script generates the module entry information and the functions for all startup and shutdown events. For the simple example implemented earlier, the module entry and functions are shown below.

```
1    /* {{{ first_test_module_entry
2     */
3    zend_module_entry first_test_module_entry =
     {
4    #if ZEND_MODULE_API_NO >= 20010901
5        STANDARD_MODULE_HEADER,
6    #endif
7        "first_test",
8        first_test_functions,
9        PHP_MINIT(first_test),
10       PHP_MSHUTDOWN(first_test),
```

```
11      PHP_RINIT(first_test),        /* Replace
    with NULL if there's nothing to do at
    request start */
12      PHP_RSHUTDOWN(first_test),   /* Replace
    with NULL if there's nothing to do at
    request end */
13      PHP_MINFO(first_test),
14  #if ZEND_MODULE_API_NO >= 20010901
15      "0.1", /* Replace with version number
    for your extension */
16  #endif
17      STANDARD_MODULE_PROPERTIES
18  };
19  /* }}} */
20  …
21  /* {{{ PHP_MINIT_FUNCTION
22   */
23  PHP_MINIT_FUNCTION(first_test)
24  {
25      /* If you have INI entries, uncomment
    these lines
26      ZEND_INIT_MODULE_GLOBALS(first_test,
    php_first_test_init_globals, NULL);
27      REGISTER_INI_ENTRIES();
28      */
29      return SUCCESS;
30  }
31  /* }}} */
32
33  /* {{{ PHP_MSHUTDOWN_FUNCTION
34   */
35  PHP_MSHUTDOWN_FUNCTION(first_test)
36  {
37      /* uncomment this line if you have INI
    entries
38      UNREGISTER_INI_ENTRIES();
39      */
40      return SUCCESS;
41  }
42  /* }}} */
43
44  /* Remove if there's nothing to do at
    request start */
45  /* {{{ PHP_RINIT_FUNCTION
46   */
47  PHP_RINIT_FUNCTION(first_test)
48  {
49      return SUCCESS;
50  }
51  /* }}} */
52
53  /* Remove if there's nothing to do at
    request end */
54  /* {{{ PHP_RSHUTDOWN_FUNCTION
55   */
```

```
56  PHP_RSHUTDOWN_FUNCTION(first_test)
57  {
58      return SUCCESS;
59  }
60  /* }}} */
```

Code Fragment 47: Extension startup and shutdown functions

As illustrated above, the *ext_skel* script generates startup and shutdown functions that are devoid of functionality, but commented to provide hints as to the type of actions to be taken within them. The following is a small contrived example to illustrate when the various functions are called.

```
1   /* {{{ PHP_MINIT_FUNCTION
2    */
3   PHP_MINIT_FUNCTION(general)
4   {
5       /* If you have INI entries, uncomment
    these lines
6       ZEND_INIT_MODULE_GLOBALS(general,
    php_general_init_globals, NULL);
7       REGISTER_INI_ENTRIES();
8       */
9       zend_printf( "In PHP_MINIT_FUNCTION\n"
    );
10      return SUCCESS;
11  }
12  /* }}} */
13
14  /* {{{ PHP_MSHUTDOWN_FUNCTION
15   */
16  PHP_MSHUTDOWN_FUNCTION(general)
17  {
18      /* uncomment this line if you have INI
    entries
19      UNREGISTER_INI_ENTRIES();
20      */
21      zend_printf( "In
    PHP_MSHUTDOWN_FUNCTION\n" );
22      return SUCCESS;
23  }
24  /* }}} */
25
26  /* Remove if there's nothing to do at
    request start */
27  /* {{{ PHP_RINIT_FUNCTION
28   */
```

```
29  PHP_RINIT_FUNCTION(general)
30  {
31      zend_printf( "In PHP_RINIT_FUNCTION\n"
    );
32      return SUCCESS;
33  }
34  /* }}} */
35
36  /* Remove if there's nothing to do at
    request end */
37  /* {{{ PHP_RSHUTDOWN_FUNCTION
38   */
39  PHP_RSHUTDOWN_FUNCTION(general)
40  {
41      zend_printf( "In
    PHP_RSHUTDOWN_FUNCTION\n" );
42      return SUCCESS;
43  }
44  /* }}} */
```

**Code Fragment 48: Extension startup and shutdown
functions, illustration**

Using the PHP script in Code Fragment 46, the
output generated is shown below. Note that in this
case the script is called using the CLI version of PHP,
not from the context of a web server.

```
1   In PHP_MINIT_FUNCTION
2   In PHP_RINIT_FUNCTION
3   [function] -> (string) execution_info
4   [file] -> (string) /home/blake/source/php-
    4.3.2/exec_info.php
5   [lineno] -> (integer) 27
6   [function] -> (string) execution_info
7   [file] -> (string) /home/blake/source/php-
    4.3.2/exec_info.php
8   [lineno] -> (integer) 23
9   In PHP_RSHUTDOWN_FUNCTION
10  In PHP_MSHUTDOWN_FUNCTION
```

**Results/Output 13: Output showing startup and shutdown
functions**

Calling User Functions

In some instances, it may be necessary to call back into the user script to perform some functionality. For example event-based programming, array walking and searching programs may require callbacks to user code. The function available for performing callbacks is defined below.

```
int call_user_function_ex(HashTable
*function_table, zval **object_pp, zval
*function_name, zval **retval_ptr_ptr, int
param_count, zval **params[], int
no_separation, HashTable *symbol_table
TSRMLS_DC)
```

The parameters of this function are described below.

HashTable *function_table	The global function table, EG(function_table), is typically used as this argument. However, if you are going to pass an object as the second argument, this can be NULL.
zval **object_pp	User object pointer. When this argument is non-null, the actual function table used is pulled from this object, so the previous argument can be NULL.
zval *function_name	Function or method name to call. The internal type of this zval argument can be a string (representing a function if the global function table is used, or a method if an object pointer is provided) or it can be an array containing an object and a string which is standard PHP notation meaning call the method of the object called string.
zval **retval_ptr_ptr	Pointer to a zval* to store the return value from the user function. The memory for this does not need to be allocated, it will be done automatically – however you must destroy the container using zval_dtor() (or a variant thereof).
int param_count	The number of arguments being sent to the user function.
zval **params[]	The arguments being sent to the user function.
int no_separation	Should the parameters be separated? This should be set to 0 generally. It may be

	slightly faster to avoid argument separation, but the function will fail if any arguments need separation.
HashTable ***symbol_table**	An alternate symbol table to be passed into the user function. Normally this is NULL which causes a default symbol table to be passed along the user function.
TSRMLS_DC	Use the TSRMLS_CC macro to provide the value for this argument.

Table 22: Arguments to the call_user_function_ex() function.

When writing functions that call the **call_user_function_ex()** function, it is useful to know whether the **function_name** argument is a valid function or method. The **zend_is_callable()** function is available to check this. The definition of this function is below:

```
zend_bool zend_is_callable(zval *callable,
zend_bool syntax_only, char **callable_name)
```

The first parameter is the **function_name** argument. The second is a flag to indicate whether to simply check syntax or check syntax and existence of the **function_name** argument. Syntactically, most strings would pass the syntax check, so this argument will usually be set to zero (false) indicating that you want to check syntax and the existence of the user function. The last parameter is a location in which to return the fully qualified function or method name represented by the first argument. This is useful in presenting error messages back to the user in case of failure. You do not need to allocate the storage for this argument, but you do need to free it.

The example for exercising the **call_user_function_ex()** function is more complex than many of the examples previously, but it is worth the effort to understand this concept. The example function accepts two parameters, the first is a PHP array, and the second is the callback function. The example simply calls back into user space passing the array key and value. The user function should return a string. The final result of the sample function is a new array consisting of the strings returned by the user function. Following is the code for the example.

```
1   PHP_FUNCTION(callback_test)
2   {
3     zval*  input_array;
4     zval*  callback_func;
5     char*  func_name;
6     int    count, i;
7     zval** args[2];
8     zval** item;
9     zval*  retval = NULL;
10
11    // make sure there are 2 args
12    if ( zend_parse_parameters(
   ZEND_NUM_ARGS() TSRMLS_CC, "zz",
   &input_array, &callback_func ) == FAILURE )
13    {
14      return;
15    }
16
17    if ( Z_TYPE_P( input_array ) != IS_ARRAY )
18    {
19      zend_error( E_WARNING, "First argument
   must be an array" );
20      return;
21    }
22
23    if ( !zend_is_callable( callback_func, 0,
   &func_name ) )
24    {
25      zend_error( E_WARNING, "Second argument
   must be a callback function or method" );
26      efree( func_name );
27      return;
28    }
29    efree( func_name );
30
31    array_init( return_value );
32
33    // get number of elements in the array
34    count = zend_hash_num_elements(
   Z_ARRVAL_P( input_array ) );
35
```

```
36    // move to the begining of the array
37    zend_hash_internal_pointer_reset(
Z_ARRVAL_P( input_array ) );
38    for ( i = 0; i < count; i ++ )
39    {
40      char*  key;
41      int    ind;
42      zval** zkey;
43
44      // get the data in the current array
element and coerce into a string
45      zend_hash_get_current_data( Z_ARRVAL_P(
input_array ), (void**) &item );
46
47      MAKE_STD_ZVAL( *zkey );
48      // get the key (note this function
returns key type)
49      if ( zend_hash_get_current_key(
Z_ARRVAL_P( input_array ), &key, &ind, 0 )
== HASH_KEY_IS_STRING )
50      {
51        ZVAL_STRING( *zkey, key, 1 );
52      }
53      else
54      {
55        ZVAL_LONG( *zkey, ind );
56      }
57
58      args[0] = zkey;
59      args[1] = item;
60
61      if ( call_user_function_ex( EG(
function_table ), NULL, callback_func,
&retval, 2, args, 0, NULL TSRMLS_CC ) ==
SUCCESS )
62      {
63        convert_to_string_ex( &retval );
64        add_next_index_string( return_value,
Z_STRVAL_P( retval ), 1 );
65        zval_dtor( retval );
66      }
67      else
68      {
69        zend_error( E_ERROR, "An error
occurred while attempting to call the user
callback" );
70        return;
71      }
72
73      zend_hash_move_forward( Z_ARRVAL_P(
input_array ) );
74    }
75  }
```

Code Fragment 49: Example using call_user_function_ex().

Lines 1 through 31 set up local variables, check the input arguments and set the return value to be of type array. Following that, the function walks through the input array similar to the example in Code Fragment 28. The key and value are obtained using the **zend_hash_get_current_key** and **zend_hash_get_current_data** functions, respectively. Lines 49 through 56 convert the returned key data to a zval. Lines 58 and 59 assign the zval arguments to the argument array that will be handed off to the user function and line 61 calls into the user function. If the call to **call_user_function_ex** is successful, then its return value (the **retval** argument) is coerced into a string and assigned to the result of this function and freed (line 63 through 65).

A sample PHP script showing the usage of this new function is below. Note that the PHP script calls this function using two standard methods for specifying a callback function. The first call simply names the function to be called using a string; the second uses the standard notation of *array(obj, string)* to denote a callback method.

```
1    <?php
2       class TestClass
3       {
4         function DoArrayWork( $key, $value )
5         {
6           return 'TestClass::DoArrayWork ('.
       $key . ' => ' . $value . ')';
7         }
8       }
9
10      function DoWork( $key, $value )
11      {
```

```
12      return 'DoWork (' . $key . ' => ' .
    $value . ')';
13    }
14
15    $array1 = array( 5, 4, 3, 2, 1 );
16    $array2 = array( 'one' => 1, 'two' => 2,
    'three' => 3, 'four' => 4, 'five' =>
17    5 );
18
19    $res_array = callback_test( $array1,
    'DoWork' );
20    print( "Results (first call):\n" .
    implode( "\n", $res_array ) . "\n\n" );
21
22    $obj = new TestClass();
23    $res_array = callback_test( $array2,
    array( $obj, 'DoArrayWork' ) );
24    print( "Results (second call):\n" .
    implode( "\n", $res_array ) . "\n\n" );
25
26    callback_test( $array1, "BogusFunc" );
27 ?>
```

Code Fragment 50: PHP script demonstrating the use of callback functions

Each instance of the callback simply returns a string consisting of the name of the function (or method) and the key and the value. The third call is to illustrate the output when attempting to use a non-existent function name as the callback function. The output is shown below.

```
1   Results (first call):
2   DoWork (0 => 5)
3   DoWork (1 => 4)
4   DoWork (2 => 3)
5   DoWork (3 => 2)
6   DoWork (4 => 1)
7
8   Results (second call):
9   TestClass::DoArrayWork (one => 1)
10  TestClass::DoArrayWork (two => 2)
11  TestClass::DoArrayWork (three => 3)
12  TestClass::DoArrayWork (four => 4)
13  TestClass::DoArrayWork (five => 5)
14
15
16  Warning: Second argument must be a callback
    function or method in
```

```
/home/blake/source/php-
4.3.2/callback_test.php on line 25
```

Results/Output 14: Results of the callback function tests.

Initialization File Support

PHP features strong initialization file support and therefore several functions and macros are exposed for use in custom extensions. The *ext_skel* script creates a framework for initialization file support that can easily be extended for use in your extension. The generated code is located in both the php_*extensionname*.h file and the *extensionname*.c file. For a test extension, simply named *general*, the generated code is shown below.

```
1    /*
2            Declare any global variables you may
     need between the BEGIN
3            and END macros here:
4
5    ZEND_BEGIN_MODULE_GLOBALS(general)
6            long   global_value;
7            char *global_string;
8    ZEND_END_MODULE_GLOBALS(general)
9    */
10
11   /* In every utility function you add that
     needs to use variables
12       in php_general_globals, call
     TSRM_FETCH(); after declaring other
13       variables used by that function, or
     better yet, pass in TSRMLS_CC
14       after the last function argument and
     declare your utility function
15       with TSRMLS_DC after the last declared
     argument.  Always refer to
16       the globals in your function as
     GENERAL_G(variable).  You are
17       encouraged to rename these macros
     something shorter, see
18       examples in any other php module
     directory.
19   */
20
```

```
21  #ifdef ZTS
22  #define GENERAL_G(v)
    TSRMG(general_globals_id,
    zend_general_globals *, v)
23  #else
24  #define GENERAL_G(v) (general_globals.v)
25  #endif
```

Code Fragment 51: INI/Globals support automatically generate by ext_skel in the ".h" file

```
1   /* If you declare any globals in
    php_general.h uncomment this:
2   ZEND_DECLARE_MODULE_GLOBALS(general)
3   */
4
5   ...
6
7   /* {{{ PHP_INI
8    */
9   /* Remove comments and fill if you need to
    have entries in php.ini
10  PHP_INI_BEGIN()
11
    STD_PHP_INI_ENTRY("general.global_value",
    "42", PHP_INI_ALL, OnUpdateInt,
    global_value, zend_general_globals,
    general_globals)
12
    STD_PHP_INI_ENTRY("general.global_string",
    "foobar", PHP_INI_ALL, OnUpdateString,
    global_string, zend_general_globals,
    general_globals)
13  PHP_INI_END()
14  */
15  /* }}} */
16
17  /* {{{ php_general_init_globals
18   */
19  /* Uncomment this function if you have INI
    entries
20  static void
    php_general_init_globals(zend_general_global
    s *general_globals)
21  {
22      general_globals->global_value = 0;
23      general_globals->global_string = NULL;
24  }
25  */
26  /* }}} */
27
28  /* {{{ PHP_MINIT_FUNCTION
29   */
```

```
30  PHP_MINIT_FUNCTION(general)
31  {
32      /* If you have INI entries, uncomment
    these lines
33      ZEND_INIT_MODULE_GLOBALS(general,
    php_general_init_globals, NULL);
34      REGISTER_INI_ENTRIES();
35      */
36      zend_printf( "In PHP_MINIT_FUNCTION\n"
    );
37      return SUCCESS;
38  }
39  /* }}} */
40
41  /* {{{ PHP_MSHUTDOWN_FUNCTION
42    */
43  PHP_MSHUTDOWN_FUNCTION(general)
44  {
45      /* uncomment this line if you have INI
    entries
46      UNREGISTER_INI_ENTRIES();
47      */
48      zend_printf( "In
    PHP_MSHUTDOWN_FUNCTION\n" );
49      return SUCCESS;
50  }
51  /* }}} */
```

Code Fragment 52: INI/Globals support automatically generate by ext_skel in the ".c" file

The code generated by the *ext_skel* script assumes that your extension will not only use initialization files, but will also need to have those variables available via easily-accessible module globals. Therefore, to fully support this mechanism, you'll need to carefully coordinate changes to both.

The automatically generated code declares a structure to store the module globals, creates an instance of that structure and initializes it. Additionally a macro is created to simplify access to the global variables. All of the INI support is initially commented so it has no effect on the module.

To begin using the initialization file support and module globals, several lines must be uncommented. These lines are all labeled in the source code and are shown in bold in the above source examples (Code Fragment 51 and Code Fragment 52). Using the default values generated by the *ext_skel* script, the following modification to the module startup function (see Code Fragment 48) shows how to access the global values.

```
1   /* {{{ PHP_MINIT_FUNCTION
2    */
3   PHP_MINIT_FUNCTION(general)
4   {
5       ZEND_INIT_MODULE_GLOBALS(general,
    php_general_init_globals, NULL);
6       zend_printf( "global_value = %d\n",
    GENERAL_G( global_value ) );
7       REGISTER_INI_ENTRIES();
8       zend_printf( "global_value = %d\n",
    GENERAL_G( global_value ) );
9
10      zend_printf( "In PHP_MINIT_FUNCTION\n"
    );
11      return SUCCESS;
12  }
13  /* }}} */
```

Code Fragment 53: Accessing INI/global values within your extension

As the above code demonstrates, when a module is first started, the globals are initialized using the **php_modulename_init_globals** function. Next the initialization file support is invoked (line 7) and the globals are set accordingly. The Zend engine sets the globals by first trying to locate the value entries in the *php.ini* file. If that file is not available or if the values are not present in that file, then the values are set to the defaults specified in the **STD_PHP_INI_ENTRY** macro (described below). The relevant output to the above example is shown below.

```
1    global_value = 0
2    global_value = 12
3    In PHP_MINIT_FUNCTION
```

Results/Output 15: Testing the INI/globals example

In the case above, the *php.ini* file contains the following lines:

```
1    [general]
2    general.global_value = 12;
```

The **STD_PHP_INI_ENTRY** (similarly defined as **STD_ZEND_INI_ENTRY**) macro is defined as:

```
1    STD_ZEND_INI_ENTRY(name, default_value,
     modifyable, on_modify, property_name,
     struct_type, struct_ptr)
```

The arguments are described in the following table.

name	The full name of the INI entry.
default_value	The default value of the entry if the *php.ini* file does not exist or does not contain this entry.
modifyable	A bitmask describing if this entry is modifyable and if so, how it is modifyable. The possible values are 0, PHP_INI_USER, PHP_INI_PERDIR, PHP_INI_SYSTEM and PHP_INI_ALL. 0 means that this value cannot be changed by the user at all. PHP_INI_USER indicates that the value can be changed at runtime by the user. PHP_INI_PERDIR indicates that the value can be set in *php.ini*, *.htaccess*, or *httpd.conf* files. PHP_INI_SYSTEM indicates that the value can only be changed via the *php.ini* or *httpd.conf* file. PHP_INI_ALL is a combination of all PHP_INI_xxx flags.

on_modify	A function pointer to a callback function that is invoked when the value is changed. There are several functions provided by the engine to use as defaults or you can write your own. This is described in more detail later.
property_name	The name of the property in the global variable structure that is associated with this INI value.
struct_type	The type of the global variable structure used to store the INI values for the module.
struct_ptr	An instance of the global structure used to store the INI values for the module.

Table 23: Arguments to the STD_PHP_INI_ENTRY macro

The standard callback functions typically used in the **on_modify** argument are OnUpdateBool, OnUpdateInt, OnUpdateReal, OnUpdateString and OnUpdateStringUnempty. Each of these functions uses the **ZEND_INI_MH** macro as a prototype. The **ZEND_INI_MH** macro is defined below:

```
#define ZEND_INI_MH(name) int
name(zend_ini_entry *entry, char *new_value,
uint new_value_length, void *mh_arg1, void
*mh_arg2, void *mh_arg3, int stage
TSRMLS_DC)
```

If you need to create your own callback function, it should use the same prototype. However, if you do want to use your own callback function, you should use one of the following macros instead of the **STD_PHP_INI_ENTRY** macro:

ZEND_INI_ENTRY(name, default_value, modifyable, on_modify)
ZEND_INI_ENTRY1(name, default_value, modifyable, on_modify, arg1)
ZEND_INI_ENTRY2(name, default_value, modifyable, on_modify,

arg1, arg2)
ZEND_INI_ENTRY3(name, default_value, modifyable, on_modify, arg1, arg2, arg3)

Table 24: Other methods for specifying INI entries

The advantage of using the **STD_PHP_INI_ENTRY** macro and the standard callback notification function is that the work of storing INI changes to globals is handled automatically. In fact, without using these tools, there is no automatic correlation between ini entries and any variables in your module.

There may be cases where you need to perform some additional work when an initialization value is changed and you therefore need your own notification handler. The macros shown above (Table 24) behave identically except that each accepts a different number of additional arguments that will simply be passed into the notification handler and are for your own internal use.

Finally, before getting to an example, there is also a set of macros available to access initialization file values directly. These are listed below.

Macro	Description
INI_INT(name)	Returns the current value of entry name as integer (long).
INI_FLT(name)	Returns the current value of entry name as float (double).
INI_STR(name)	Returns the current value of entry name as string. Note: This string is not duplicated, but instead points to internal data. Further access requires duplication to local memory.
INI_BOOL(name)	Returns the current value of entry name as Boolean (defined as zend_bool, which

	currently means unsigned char).
INI_ORIG_INT(name)	Returns the original value of entry name as integer (long).
INI_ORIG_FLT(name)	Returns the original value of entry name as float (double).
INI_ORIG_STR(name)	Returns the original value of entry name as string. Note: This string is not duplicated, but instead points to internal data. Further access requires duplication to local memory.
INI_ORIG_BOOL(name)	Returns the original value of entry name as Boolean (defined as zend_bool, which currently means unsigned char).

Table 25: Macros for accessing ini entries directly.

The example for illustrating all of the above functionality is again quite complex. Changes to both the ".c" and the ".h" files are required. These changes are shown below.

```
1    ZEND_BEGIN_MODULE_GLOBALS(general)
2            long  global_value;
3            char *global_string;
4            char *test_string1;
5            char *test_string3;
6    ZEND_END_MODULE_GLOBALS(general)
7
8    ZEND_API ZEND_INI_MH(OnUpdateNoGlobal);
9    ZEND_API ZEND_INI_MH(OnUpdateTestString);
```

Code Fragment 54: Relevant changes to php_general.h to illustrate INI/globals implementations.

The changes to the header file are first to provide a storage location for the globals. Note that there is a storage location for test_string1 and test_string3 but not test_string2. This is because the initialization file entry for test_string2 includes a custom change notification handler that does not update the globals. The other relevant change above are lines 8 and 9 which declare two new change notification handlers.

```
1    /* {{{ PHP_INI
2     */
3    PHP_INI_BEGIN()
4
     STD_PHP_INI_ENTRY("general.global_value",
     "42", PHP_INI_ALL, OnUpdateInt,
     global_value, zend_general_globals,
     general_globals)
5
     STD_PHP_INI_ENTRY("general.global_string",
     "foobar", PHP_INI_ALL, OnUpdateString,
     global_string, zend_general_globals,
     general_globals)
6
     STD_PHP_INI_ENTRY("general.test_string1",
     "test_string_1", PHP_INI_ALL,
     OnUpdateTestString, test_string1,
     zend_general_globals, general_globals)
7        PHP_INI_ENTRY1("general.test_string2",
     "test_string_2", PHP_INI_ALL,
     OnUpdateNoGlobal, "some random value")
8
     STD_PHP_INI_ENTRY("general.test_string3",
     "test_string_3", PHP_INI_SYSTEM,
     OnUpdateString, test_string3,
     zend_general_globals, general_globals)
9    PHP_INI_END()
10   /* }}} */
11
12   /* {{{ php_general_init_globals
13    */
14   static void
     php_general_init_globals(zend_general_global
     s *general_globals)
15   {
16       general_globals->global_value = 0;
17       general_globals->global_string = NULL;
18       general_globals->test_string1 = NULL;
19       general_globals->test_string3 = NULL;
20   }
21   /* }}} */
22
23   ...
24
25   ZEND_API ZEND_INI_MH(OnUpdateTestString)
26   {
27     zend_printf( "updating ini value '%s' to
     '%s'\n", entry->name, new_value );
28     OnUpdateString( entry, new_value,
     new_value_length, mh_arg1, mh_arg2, mh_arg3,
     stage TSRMLS_CC );
29
30     return SUCCESS;
```

```
31  }
32
33  ZEND_API ZEND_INI_MH(OnUpdateNoGlobal)
34  {
35    zend_printf( "updating ini value '%s' to
      '%s' with user arg1 = '%s'\n", entry->name,
      new_value, (char*) mh_arg1 );
36
37    return SUCCESS;
38  }
39
40  PHP_FUNCTION(ini_global_print)
41  {
42    zend_printf( "Global Values:\n" );
43    zend_printf( "  global_value  = %d\n",
      GENERAL_G( global_value   ) );
44    zend_printf( "  global_string = '%s'\n",
      GENERAL_G( global_string  ) );
45    zend_printf( "  test_string1  = '%s'\n",
      GENERAL_G( test_string1   ) );
46    zend_printf( "  test_string3  = '%s'\n",
      GENERAL_G( test_string3   ) );
47    zend_printf( "\n\n" );
48
49    zend_printf( "Ini Values:\n" );
50    zend_printf( "  global_value  = %d
      (originally %d)\n", INI_INT(
      "general.global_value" ), INI_ORIG_INT(
      "general.global_value"  ) );
51    zend_printf( "  global_string = '%s'
      (originally '%s')\n", INI_STR(
      "general.global_string" ), INI_ORIG_STR(
      "general.global_string" ) );
52    zend_printf( "  test_string1 = '%s'
      (originally '%s')\n", INI_STR(
      "general.test_string1" ), INI_ORIG_STR(
      "general.test_string1" )  );
53    zend_printf( "  test_string2 = '%s'
      (originally '%s')\n", INI_STR(
      "general.test_string2" ), INI_ORIG_STR(
      "general.test_string2" )  );
54    zend_printf( "  test_string3 = '%s'
      (originally '%s')\n", INI_STR(
      "general.test_string3" ), INI_ORIG_STR(
      "general.test_string3" )  );
55    zend_printf( "\n\n" );
56  }
```

Code Fragment 55: Relevant changes to general.c to illustrate INI/globals implementations.

The first changes to the implementation file are lines 6 through 8 where three new initialization file entries are defined. The first is *general.test_string1* which is a standard string entry with a custom change notification handler. The second is *general.test_string2* which is a completely custom entry shown for illustration. In this definition, changes to *general.test_string2* will be passed to the change notification function **OnUpdateNoGlobal** and the value passed into that function's **mh_arg1** argument is the static string, "some random value". In a real-world implementation this would likely be a pointer to an object or structure where the new value would be stored. The third new ini entry is *general.test_string3* which is defined in the standard way except that its **modifyable** argument is set to PHP_INI_SYSTEM.

Lines 14 through 20 above show the initialization of the new global variables.

Lines 25 through 31 illustrate how to write a change notification handler that does some custom work (printing some feedback) and then calls the standard **OnUpdateString** handler to update the global variable value. Without the call to **OnUpdateString**, the ini value would be updated, but the global variable would not.

Lines 33 through 38 are the implementation of the second change notification handler. This one, **OnUpdateNoGlobal**, simply prints out some information, showing the concept of a completely custom handler.

Lines 40 through 56 are the implementation of a new extension function **ini_global_print()** that simply prints out all of the modules global variables and ini

entries. The PHP test script used to exercise all of
the above functionality is below.

```
1   <?php
2     error_reporting( E_ALL );
3
4     ini_global_print();
5     ini_set( 'general.test_string1', 'new
      value 1' );
6     ini_global_print();
7     ini_set( 'general.test_string2', 'new
      value 2' );
8     ini_global_print();
9     ini_set( 'general.test_string3', 'new
      value 3' );
10    ini_global_print();
11  ?>
```

**Code Fragment 56: PHP script for testing the INI/globals
functions.**

This simple example is used in conjunction with the
following *php.ini* file:

```
1   [general]
2   general.global_value = 12;
3   general.test_string3 = "Hello from php.ini";
```

The output of the above script is:

```
1   In PHP_MINIT_FUNCTION
2   global_value = 0
3   updating ini value 'general.test_string1' to
    'test_string_1'
4   updating ini value 'general.test_string2' to
    'test_string_2' with user arg1 = 'some
    random value'
5   global_value = 12
6   In PHP_RINIT_FUNCTION
7   Global Values:
8     global_value  = 12
9     global_string = 'foobar'
10    test_string1  = 'test_string_1'
11    test_string3  = 'Hello from php.ini'
12
13
14  Ini Values:
15    global_value  = 12 (originally 12)
```

```
16    global_string = 'foobar' (originally
      'foobar')
17    test_string1 = 'test_string_1' (originally
      'test_string_1')
18    test_string2 = 'test_string_2' (originally
      'test_string_2')
19    test_string3 = 'Hello from php.ini'
      (originally 'Hello from php.ini')
20
21
22 updating ini value 'general.test_string1' to
   'new value 1'
23 Global Values:
24    global_value  = 12
25    global_string = 'foobar'
26    test_string1  = 'new value 1'
27    test_string3  = 'Hello from php.ini'
28
29
30 Ini Values:
31    global_value  = 12 (originally 12)
32    global_string = 'foobar' (originally
      'foobar')
33    test_string1 = 'new value 1' (originally
      'test_string_1')
34    test_string2 = 'test_string_2' (originally
      'test_string_2')
35    test_string3 = 'Hello from php.ini'
      (originally 'Hello from php.ini')
36
37
38 updating ini value 'general.test_string2' to
   'new value 2' with user arg1 = 'some random
   value'
39 Global Values:
40    global_value  = 12
41    global_string = 'foobar'
42    test_string1  = 'new value 1'
43    test_string3  = 'Hello from php.ini'
44
45
46 Ini Values:
47    global_value  = 12 (originally 12)
48    global_string = 'foobar' (originally
      'foobar')
49    test_string1 = 'new value 1' (originally
      'test_string_1')
50    test_string2 = 'new value 2' (originally
      'test_string_2')
51    test_string3 = 'Hello from php.ini'
      (originally 'Hello from php.ini')
52
53
54 Global Values:
55    global_value  = 12
```

```
56    global_string = 'foobar'
57    test_string1  = 'new value 1'
58    test_string3  = 'Hello from php.ini'
59
60
61  Ini Values:
62    global_value  = 12 (originally 12)
63    global_string = 'foobar' (originally
      'foobar')
64    test_string1 = 'new value 1' (originally
      'test_string_1')
65    test_string2 = 'new value 2' (originally
      'test_string_2')
66    test_string3 = 'Hello from php.ini'
      (originally 'Hello from php.ini')
67
68
69  In PHP_RSHUTDOWN_FUNCTION
70  updating ini value 'general.test_string1' to
      'test_string_1'
71  updating ini value 'general.test_string2' to
      'test_string_2' with user arg1 = 'some
      random value'
72  In PHP_MSHUTDOWN_FUNCTION
```

Results/Output 16: Output from the INI/globals test.

Output highlighted in bold text above is not related to functionality just added, but is the result of other examples in this document. It is included to illustrate some interesting aspects of how PHP handles initialization files. Particularly interesting is that PHP resets the ini entries in the context of the PHP_MSHUTDOWN_FUNCTION.

Otherwise the output is as expected. The first set of output (lines 7 through 21) show the state of the globals and the ini values as initialized. Next, lines 22 through 37 show that both the global value and ini value are properly updated by the PHP call, *ini_set('general.test_string1', 'new value 1')*.

Lines 38 through 53 show that the ini value is properly updated by the PHP call *ini_set('general.test_string2', 'new value 2')*. Finally, lines 54 through 68 show that nothing is changed by the PHP call *ini_set('general.test_string3', 'new value 3')* which is expected because this entry should not be modifiable via user code.

Classes

Since PHP is moving toward a more object oriented approach, I suspect that more and more extensions will provide internal classes in conjunction with or as a replacement to the standard procedural programming model of PHP. Creating and exposing an internal class to the end user is somewhat complex, almost completely undocumented and still a bit immature (in terms of overall functionality), but the OO model is rapidly expanding in PHP. In fact the beta version of PHP 5 is available and already the differences in the object model make creating extension classes more obvious. This fact should be noted and while much of the information here will not change in version 5 of PHP, some will and some re-work will likely need to be done if you plan to release a custom extension class for version 5.

At the basic level, exposing a custom class is similar in many respects to using objects as described above. The key differences are:

1. To provide a complete internal class from which an object can be created using the *new classname()* syntax
2. To implement an internal constructor that is automatically called when an object is created
3. To provide methods of the class

If you are planning to build a new class-based extension from scratch, I suggest starting by identifying the objects and methods you wish to provide and developing a procedural view of these items that can be used with the *ext_skel* script.

For example, assume you want to create two new classes, **MyClass** and **MySubClass** where the latter is not a proper OO subclass, but a member object of the former. The **MyClass** object will contain two methods, **return_int()** and **return_string()** and will expose three properties, **intval, stringval** and **objval**. The **MyClass** object will provide a constructor. The **MySubClass** object will also contain two methods, **return_int()** and **return_string()** and two properties, **intval** and **stringval**. The **MySubClass** object will not provide a constructor and will only be created internally by the **MyClass** constructor and available through the **objval** property.

Start by identifying all of the required methods. Then, using a simple *classname_methodname* format, create a prototype file (for the *ext_skel*) script that contains the methods in a procedural format. For example, the following illustrates the example above.

```
1    object myclass( string arg1, int arg2 )
     Create object of myclass
2    int    myclass_return_int( void )
3    string myclass_return_string( void )
4    int    mysubclass_return_int( void )
5    string mysubclass_return_string( void )
```

Code Fragment 57: Prototype file, myclass.proto

Using the *ext_skel* script with this file will produce a standard set of functions that begin the process of exposing a class from a custom module. It is not required that you use the *ext_skel* script in any custom module, but the coding work performed by the script is immense and simplifies the work in general. Once the skeleton has been developed, the real work of exposing the new classes begins.

```
1   #include "php.h"
2   #include "php_ini.h"
3   #include "ext/standard/info.h"
4   #include "php_myclass.h"
5
6   static zend_class_entry
    *myclass_class_entry_ptr;
7   static zend_class_entry
    *mysubclass_class_entry_ptr;
8
9   /* If you declare any globals in
    php_myclass.h uncomment this:
10  ZEND_DECLARE_MODULE_GLOBALS(myclass)
11  */
12
13  /* True global resources - no need for
    thread safety here */
14  static int le_myclass;
15
16  /* {{{ myclass_functions[]
17   *
18   * Every user visible function must have an
    entry in myclass_functions[].
19   */
20  function_entry myclass_functions[] = {
21      PHP_FE(confirm_myclass_compiled,
    NULL)          /* For testing, remove later. */
22      PHP_FE(myclass_init,     NULL)
23      PHP_FE(myclass_mysubclass,  NULL)
24      PHP_FE(myclass_return_int,  NULL)
25      PHP_FE(myclass_return_string,   NULL)
26      PHP_FE(mysubclass_return_int,   NULL)
27      PHP_FE(mysubclass_return_string,
    NULL)
28      {NULL, NULL, NULL}  /* Must be the last
    line in myclass_functions[] */
29  };
30  /* }}} */
31
32  function_entry myclass_class_functions[] = {
33      PHP_FALIAS(myclass, myclass_init, NULL)
34      PHP_FALIAS(return_int,
    myclass_return_int, NULL)
35      PHP_FALIAS(return_string,
    myclass_return_string, NULL)
36      {NULL, NULL, NULL}
37  };
```

```
38
39  function_entry mysubclass_class_functions[]
    = {
40      PHP_FALIAS(return_int,
    mysubclass_return_int, NULL)
41      PHP_FALIAS(return_string,
    mysubclass_return_string, NULL)
42      {NULL, NULL, NULL}
43  };
```

Code Fragment 58: Implementation of myclass (myclass.c) section 1

The first section above illustrates the first set of changes made to the implementation file, myclass.c. Note that modifications to the source (lines not generated by *ext_skel*) are shown in bold. Lines 6 and 7 declare to static variables of type **zend_class_entry*** that will be used later in the module initialization to expose the classes. Lines 32 through 43 show two new function entry blocks not normally used in a procedural module. Both function entry blocks use the **PHP_FALIAS** macro rather than the **PHP_FE** macro to provide entries to the function entry array. The **PHP_FALIAS** macro accepts three arguments, a function alias name, the function to alias and the argument types macro (same as for the **PHP_FE** macro).

The first block (lines 32 through 37), **myclass_class_functions**, is the list of methods that will be available to the **MyClass** class. For example, the **MyClass** class will have a method called **myclass** that is an alias to the **myclass_init** function. The second block (lines 39 through 43), **mysubclass_class_functions**, is the list of methods that will be available to the **MySubClass** class.

I should note that it is not absolutely necessary to use the aliasing mechanism above to map methods to functions. It is possible to simply use the **PHP_FE** macro within a function entry block that will describe the methods of a class. However, using the above method can simplify development (with the *ext_skel* script and can also be used to provide both an OO method and a procedural method of access to your extension simultaneously.

```
1    PHP_MINIT_FUNCTION(myclass)
2    {
3        zend_class_entry myclass_class_entry;
4        zend_class_entry mysubclass_class_entry;
5
6        INIT_CLASS_ENTRY( myclass_class_entry,
     "myclass", myclass_class_functions );
7        INIT_CLASS_ENTRY(
     mysubclass_class_entry, "mysubclass",
     mysubclass_class_functions );
8        myclass_class_entry_ptr =
     zend_register_internal_class(
     &myclass_class_entry TSRMLS_CC );
9        mysubclass_class_entry_ptr =
     zend_register_internal_class(
     &mysubclass_class_entry TSRMLS_CC );
10
11       /* If you have INI entries, uncomment
     these lines
12       ZEND_INIT_MODULE_GLOBALS(myclass,
     php_myclass_init_globals, NULL);
13       REGISTER_INI_ENTRIES();
14       */
15       return SUCCESS;
16   }
```

Code Fragment 59: Implementation of myclass (myclass.c) section 2

The next relevant change to the source is shown above (Code Fragment 59). The module initialization function is used to register the class with PHP. The **INIT_CLASS_ENTRY** macro accepts three arguments, a temporary variable for initializing the internal class structure, a name for the new class, and the name of the function entry block to be used with the class. Because of the way that the Zend engine works with class names, I strongly recommend that you use all lowercase characters in the name of the class you pass to this macro. This will be explained in more detail later.

After the **INIT_CLASS_ENTRY** macro is called for each internal class, the **zend_register_internal_class()** function is called. This function takes the temporary **zend_class_entry** variable and TSRMLS_CC as its arguments. It returns a fully registered **zend_class_entry*** that will be used to initialize new zval containers later. The return value from **zend_register_internal_class()** function should be stored globally in your module.

Now it is time to fill out the implementation of all of the internal functions for the extension. The first that will be considered is the **myclass_init()** function. Note that this function has an alias name **myclass** (see line 33 of Code Fragment 58). When a new object is created, the engine searches for a function with the same name as the class to use as an object constructor. By creating the aforementioned alias, there is a function that exactly matches the name of the class and is therefore considered to be the constructor of the class. One caveat of this method is that Zend searches for a function (or alias) with a name matching exactly (case sensitive match) the name of the class provided in the **INIT_CLASS_ENTRY** macro. However, when the engine attempts to invoke the function, it expects a lower-case function name to be present. Therefore if you use a mixed case name in the **INIT_CLASS_ENTRY** macro, then you'll have to provide a mixed-case alias in the function entry table to represent the constructor. However, when the engine attempts to invoke that function, it will have converted the name to all lower-case letters and will not find that function and generate a warning. If you feel strongly about using a mixed case name, you can provide two aliases to the same function, such as in the following.

```
1    function_entry myclass_class_functions[] = {
2        PHP_FALIAS(MyClass, myclass_init, NULL)
3        PHP_FALIAS(myclass, myclass_init, NULL)
4        PHP_FALIAS(return_int,
     myclass_return_int, NULL)
5        PHP_FALIAS(return_string,
     myclass_return_string, NULL)
6        {NULL, NULL, NULL}
7    };
```

The above function entry table will allow *INIT_CLASS_ENTRY(myclass_class_entry, "MyClass", myclass_class_functions)* to work as expected.

```
1    /* {{{ proto object myclass(string arg1, int
     arg2)
2       Create object of myclass */
3    PHP_FUNCTION(myclass_init)
4    {
5        char *arg1 = NULL;
6        int argc = ZEND_NUM_ARGS();
7        int arg1_len;
8        long arg2;
9        zval* obj;
10
11       if ( !getThis() )
12       {
13           zend_error( E_ERROR,
     "'myclass_init()' cannot be called directly.
     use new MyClass() instead" );
14       }
15
16       zend_printf( "Wow!  I'm in the
     'constructor', myclass_init.\n" );
17
18       if (zend_parse_parameters(argc
     TSRMLS_CC, "sl", &arg1, &arg1_len, &arg2) ==
     FAILURE)
19           return;
20
```

```
21      MAKE_STD_ZVAL( obj );
22      object_init_ex( obj,
   mysubclass_class_entry_ptr );
23      add_property_string( obj, "stringval",
   "internal string", 1 );
24      add_property_long  ( obj, "intval",
   123456 );
25
26      object_init_ex( getThis(),
   myclass_class_entry_ptr );
27      add_property_string( getThis(),
   "stringval", arg1, 1 );
28      add_property_long  ( getThis(),
   "intval", arg2 );
29      add_property_zval  ( getThis(),
   "objval", obj );
30  }
31  /* }}} */
32
33  /* {{{ proto int ()
34     myclass_return_int( void ) */
35  PHP_FUNCTION(myclass_return_int)
36  {
37      zval** tmp;
38
39      if (ZEND_NUM_ARGS() != 0) {
40          WRONG_PARAM_COUNT;
41      }
42
43      if ( zend_hash_find( Z_OBJPROP_P(
   getThis() ), "intval", sizeof( "intval" ),
   (void**) &tmp ) == SUCCESS )
44      {
45          *return_value = **tmp;
46          zval_copy_ctor( return_value );
47      }
48      else
49      {
50          zend_error( E_ERROR, "Critical
   failure, 'intval' property not found in
   object" );
51      }
52  }
53  /* }}} */
54
55  /* {{{ proto string myclass_return_string()
56     */
57  PHP_FUNCTION(myclass_return_string)
58  {
59      zval** tmp;
60
61      if (ZEND_NUM_ARGS() != 0) {
62          WRONG_PARAM_COUNT;
63      }
64
```

```
65     if ( zend_hash_find( Z_OBJPROP_P(
   getThis() ), "stringval", sizeof(
   "stringval" ), (void**) &tmp ) == SUCCESS )
66     {
67         *return_value = **tmp;
68         zval_copy_ctor( return_value );
69     }
70     else
71     {
72         zend_error( E_ERROR, "Critical
   failure, 'stringval' property not found in
   object" );
73     }
74 }
75 /* }}} */
76
77 /* {{{ proto int ()
78    mysubclass_return_int( void ) */
79 PHP_FUNCTION(mysubclass_return_int)
80 {
81     zval** tmp;
82     zval** tmp2;
83
84     if (ZEND_NUM_ARGS() != 0) {
85         WRONG_PARAM_COUNT;
86     }
87
88     if ( zend_hash_find( Z_OBJPROP_P(
   getThis() ), "intval", sizeof( "intval" ),
   (void**) &tmp ) == SUCCESS )
89     {
90         *return_value = **tmp;
91         zval_copy_ctor( return_value );
92     }
93     else
94     {
95         zend_error( E_ERROR, "Critical
   failure, 'intval' property not found in
   object" );
96     }
97 }
98 /* }}} */
99
100 /* {{{ proto string
   mysubclass_return_string()
101     */
102 PHP_FUNCTION(mysubclass_return_string)
103 {
104     zval** tmp;
105     zval** tmp2;
106
107     if (ZEND_NUM_ARGS() != 0) {
108         WRONG_PARAM_COUNT;
109     }
110
```

```
111    if ( zend_hash_find( Z_OBJPROP_P(
    getThis() ), "stringval", sizeof(
    "stringval" ), (void**) &tmp ) == SUCCESS )
112    {
113          *return_value = **tmp;
114          zval_copy_ctor( return_value );
115    }
116    else
117    {
118          zend_error( E_ERROR, "Critical
    failure, 'stringval' property not found in
    object" );
119    }
120 }
121 /* }}} */
```

Code Fragment 60: Implementation of myclass (myclass.c) section 3

The most interesting function illustrated above is the **myclass_init()** function. It is the *constructor* function that will be called when a new instance of **MyClass** is created. The most important new concept introduced in this function is the use of the **getThis()** function. **getThis()** returns the *$this* pointer for the class when this internal function is used in the context of an object. Using **getThis()**, it is possible to know how the user is invoking this function within their PHP code. If the user is attempting to simply call directly into the **myclass_init()** function, there will be no *$this* pointer and the **getThis()** function will return NULL. However, if the user is correctly instantiating an object using the *$obj = new MyClass(...)* syntax, the *$this* pointer will be available and the **getThis()** function will return its zval container. In fact, lines 11 through 14 illustrate exactly this idea and disallow invoking the **myclass_init()** function directly from PHP.

Lines 21 through 24 create the sub-object that will be available to the return object. This sub-object is of type **MySubClass** as described above. The

MAKE_STD_ZVAL macro has been discussed previously, but the **object_init_ex()** function in this context has not. The **object_init_ex()** function accepts two arguments, a **zval*** and a **zend_class_entry***. The first is the container that should be initialized, the second is the result of a previous call to **zend_register_internal_class()** as described above. In the example, the object is initialized using **mysubclass_class_entry_ptr** which is the fully-qualified class entry for the **MySubClass** class. The properties of the new object are set in line 23 and 24 (using static values for this example).

Lines 26 through 29 initialize and return the main object. Note that this function does not return its value through the standard **return_value** variable, but through the *$this* variable using **getThis()**. If you return a class via the **return_value** variable, the result will be that the *$this* variable (on the PHP side) will be uninitialized.

All of the remaining functions are essentially the same, so an explanation of only one will be given here. The **myclass_return_int()** function (lines 33 through 53) show how to return values from objects using **zend_hash_find()** and **getThis()** together. In this function, the property *intval* is located and its zval container is copied to the return value using the **zval_copy_ctor()** function. If the *intval* property is not found, an error is generated.

One nice item to note about this methodology is that Zend provides the right *$this* value for the context of the function call. As is clear, there is nothing different at all in the implementation of **myclass_return_int** and **mysubclass_return_int**. A

PHP script illustrating all of the concepts in this example follows.

```
1    <?php
2      $aClass  = new MyClass( "string", 2 );
3      $aClass2 = new MyClass( "string", 2 );
4      var_dump( $aClass );
5
6      print( "aClass->return_int() = " .
    $aClass->return_int() . "\n" );
7      print( "aClass->return_string() = " .
    $aClass->return_string() . "\n" );
8
9      $aClass->objval->stringval = "hello,
    world";
10     print( "aSubClass->return_int() = " .
    $aClass->objval->return_int() . "\n" );
11     print( "aSubClass->return_string() = " .
    $aClass->objval->return_string() . "\n" );
12
13     $aClass2->objval->stringval = "oh no!";
14     var_dump( $aClass2 );
15     print( "aSubClass->return_int() = " .
    $aClass2->objval->return_int() . "\n" );
16     print( "aSubClass->return_string() = " .
    $aClass2->objval->return_string() . "\n" );
17
18     print( "aSubClass->return_int() = " .
    $aClass->objval->return_int() . "\n" );
19     print( "aSubClass->return_string() = " .
    $aClass->objval->return_string() . "\n" );
20   ?>
```

Code Fragment 61: PHP script illustrating the internal class implementation.

The PHP script shows how multiple objects of the same class can be constructed and how, because of the method of implementation, the properties can be accessed directly or through the access functions provided. Most notable is fact that *$aClass >objval* correctly returns an object which can be used as such.

```
1    Wow!  I'm in the 'constructor',
    myclass_init.
2    Wow!  I'm in the 'constructor',
    myclass_init.
3    object(myclass)(3) {
```

```
 4     ["stringval"]=>
 5     string(6) "string"
 6     ["intval"]=>
 7     int(2)
 8     ["objval"]=>
 9     object(mysubclass)(2) {
10       ["stringval"]=>
11       string(15) "internal string"
12       ["intval"]=>
13       int(123456)
14     }
15   }
16   aClass->return_int() = 2
17   aClass->return_string() = string
18   aSubClass->return_int() = 123456
19   aSubClass->return_string() = hello, world
20   object(myclass)(3) {
21     ["stringval"]=>
22     string(6) "string"
23     ["intval"]=>
24     int(2)
25     ["objval"]=>
26     object(mysubclass)(2) {
27       ["stringval"]=>
28       string(6) "oh no!"
29       ["intval"]=>
30       int(123456)
31     }
32   }
33   aSubClass->return_int() = 123456
34   aSubClass->return_string() = oh no!
35   aSubClass->return_int() = 123456
36   aSubClass->return_string() = hello, world
```

Results/Output 17: Results from the internal class test PHP script.

While the above classes are simplistic, the concepts for introducing new classes into PHP are illustrated. As PHP moves to become a more object oriented programming language, providing classes in modules will become much more necessary. The full example later in this document will illustrate how to provide a clean procedural and OO extension simultaneously.

Full Example

To illustrate a complete example of a PHP extension, a good set of new functionality must be identified and implemented in C. Alternately, one could identify an existing C package (for example, an open source library) to be ported to PHP. For this example, I will be incorporating the GLPK (GNU Linear Programming Kit) into PHP. The GLPK is a toolkit for solving large-scale linear programming (LP) and mixed integer programming (MIP) problems. If you are not familiar with this type of mathematical problem, suffice it so say that the toolkit is designed to solve complex mathematical problems dealing with optimization. Detailed information about the GLPK can be found at http://www.gnu.org/software/glpk/glpk.html. A full understanding of the toolkit is not required to appreciate this example.

There is more than one approach that may be considered when mapping a C library (such as GLPK) to PHP. The first and most obvious approach is to simply map the C function calls directly to PHP. While this approach accomplishes the objective of providing a PHP extension to the library, it misses some of the power of using the PHP language. For example, in the GLPK, there is a C function, **lpx_set_row_name()** that accepts three parameters, the problem pointer, the row number, and the row name, respectively. Without going into detail about GLPK specifics, it is obvious that if a particular problem consists of dozens or hundreds of rows, the aforementioned function must be called that number of times. A more PHP-like approach to this would be to provide a function that accepts an array of strings

representing the row names in ascending order.
From a readability perspective, the code is improved
(see below).

```
1    // example setting 4 row names using C
2    lpx_set_row_name( lp, 1, "row 1" );
3    lpx_set_row_name( lp, 2, "row 2" );
4    lpx_set_row_name( lp, 3, "row 3" );
5    lpx_set_row_name( lp, 4, "row 4" );
6
7    // example using a more PHP-like function
8    glpk_set_row_names( lp, array( "row 1", "row
     2", "row 3", "row 4" ) );
9
```

Note that the decisions on implementation are
completely yours. Mapping C to PHP directly may be
the best decision for the particular extension.
Because of the way that I typically use an LP solver, I
will be building an interface that represents my
expectations.

The GLPK provides nearly 100 API functions. This
example will not attempt to map all functions, nor
will it provide 100% coverage of all the functionality
in the GLPK. Again, this example is primarily to
illustrate the development of an extension and
secondarily to meet my personal need of having a
LP/MIP solver in PHP.

In fact, this extension is going to provide the
following PHP functions:

```
1    glpk_create
2    glpk_set_row_names
3    glpk_set_col_names
4    glpk_set_row_bound
5    glpk_set_col_bound
6    glpk_set_matrix
7    glpk_set_obj_coeffs
8    glpk_solve
9    glpk_delete
10   glpk_set_coltype
```

The above 16 functions will cover nearly 60 - 70% of all the functionality in the GLPK. This is primarily due to the fact that most of the other GLPK functions will only be used internally and so they are not required at the PHP level. Also, many utility functions for reading and writing different types of problem description files are not included in this example. Some unimplemented extension functions are named in the code, but not discussed here.

This extension will also expose a class, so that the GLPK functionality can be used in an OO fashion within PHP. The class will be called **GLPKProblem** and will provide the following methods:

```
1   new GLPKProblem
2   GLPKProblem->SetRowNames
3   GLPKProblem->SetColNames
4   GLPKProblem->SetRowBound
5   GLPKProblem->SetColBound
6   GLPKProblem->SetMatrix
7   GLPKProblem->SetObjCoeffs
8   GLPKProblem->Solve
9   GLPKProblem->Delete
10  GLPKProblem->SetColType
```

Because this extension will provide a procedural and an OO interface simultaneously, the parameter list for each function is variable. In the procedural case, the first parameter of each of the functions above will be a resource representing the internal problem structure. In the OO case, each method will use the *$this* pointer to store the resource and therefore the first parameter to each method will **not** be a resource identifier. Because of this, I will not provide the argument types in the function prototype file used by *ext_skel,* but only the function names.

GLPK Extension: config.m4

To begin, I created a file called *glpk.proto* containing the function list above. After running the *ext_skel* script, the first file to modify is, of course, the *config.m4* file. Since this extension uses an external library, more changes to this file are required than in the previous example. The file (commented lines deleted) is shown below.

```
1   PHP_ARG_WITH(glpk, for glpk support,
2   [  --with-glpk              Include glpk
    support])
3
4   if test "$PHP_GLPK" != "no"; then
5     SEARCH_PATH="/usr/local /usr"     # you
    might want to change this
6     SEARCH_FOR="/include/glpk.h"  # you most
    likely want to change this
7     if test -r $PHP_GLPK/; then # path given
    as parameter
8       GLPK_DIR=$PHP_GLPK
9     else # search default path list
10      AC_MSG_CHECKING([for glpk files in
    default path])
11      for i in $SEARCH_PATH ; do
12        if test -r $i/$SEARCH_FOR; then
13          GLPK_DIR=$i
14          AC_MSG_RESULT(found in $i)
15        fi
16      done
17    fi
18    dnl
19    if test -z "$GLPK_DIR"; then
20      AC_MSG_RESULT([not found])
21      AC_MSG_ERROR([Please reinstall the glpk
    distribution])
22    fi
23
24    # --with-glpk -> add include path
25    PHP_ADD_INCLUDE($GLPK_DIR/include)
26
27    dnl # --with-glpk -> chech for lib and
    symbol presence
28    LIBNAME=glpk # you may want to change this
29    LIBSYMBOL=glp_lpx_read_model # you most
    likely want to change this
30
31    PHP_CHECK_LIBRARY($LIBNAME,$LIBSYMBOL,
```

```
32      [
33          PHP_ADD_LIBRARY_WITH_PATH($LIBNAME,
    $GLPK_DIR/lib, GLPK_SHARED_LIBADD)
34          AC_DEFINE(HAVE_GLPKLIB,1,[ ])
35      ],[
36          AC_MSG_ERROR([wrong glpk lib version or
    lib not found])
37      ],[
38      ])
39
40      PHP_SUBST(GLPK_SHARED_LIBADD)
41
42      PHP_NEW_EXTENSION(glpk, glpk.c,
    $ext_shared)
43  fi
```

Code Fragment 62: config.m4 for the GLPK extension

The *config.m4* file above is much more complex than the ones previously described. This is primarily due to the fact that the GLPK extension requires an external library, and so more checks are required to ensure that the library and its associated header files are available to the PHP build system. When configuring PHP with GLPK support, the configure line will be specified as in the example below:

```
1   ./configure --with-glpk=/path/to/glpk
```

When the above format is used, an internal variable **$PHP_GLPK** is set to the value to the right of the equal ('=') sign. In the above example **$PHP_GLPK** would be literally set to '/path/to/glpk'. Line 4 of the *config.m4* file checks to see if the **$PHP_GLPK** variable is equal to the string 'no'. If it is so, no more lines are processed related to GLPK. Otherwise, line 7 checks to see if the directory **$PHP_GLPK** exists. If so, the **$GLPK_DIR** variable is set to the value of **$PHP_GLPK**. If not, lines 7 through 16 are a loop in which the directories specified in **$SEARCH_PATH** are searched for the file specified by $SEARCH_FOR. In this the the

$SEARCH_FOR variable is '/include/glpk.h', so if this file is found, the directory in which it was found is assigned to **$GLPK_DIR**.

By the time the script runs through to line 19, the correct directory for GLPK should be assigned to **$GLPK_DIR**. The script checks again to ensure that the value of the variable is an existing directory and exits with a warning if it is not. Line 25 then adds the GLPK includes directory to the list of include directories required to compile PHP.

Next the script checks for the existence of the *glp_lpx_read_model* symbol within the GLPK library using the PHP_CHECK_LIBRARY macro (see Table 7). This symbol was picked because this function was added to the GLPK library in the version 4.0 release. If a library with the same name did exist, but did not contain the symbol specified, this check would cause the *configure* script to fail with a warning. If the library is found and the specified symbol exists, then the library is added to the list of libraries required to build PHP.

GLPK Extension: Implementation

Without delving into the details of LP/MIP concepts, it is important to understand how the solver engine works at a high level. First a problem object must be created and initialized. Next, the problem object parameters are set. Next, the problem is described via function calls passing the problem object. Next, the problem is solved using a function call, again passing the problem object. Finally, the results (solution) of the problem are obtained via function calls.

The following C sample is included with the GLPK distribution to show standard usage for a simplistic problem.

```
1    /* sample.c */
2
3    #include <stdio.h>
4    #include <stdlib.h>
5    #include "glpk.h"
6
7    int main(void)
8    {       LPX *lp;
9            int rn[1+9], cn[1+9];
10           double a[1+9], Z, x1, x2, x3;
11
12   s1:     lp = lpx_create_prob();
13   s2:     lpx_set_prob_name(lp, "sample");
14
15   s3:     lpx_add_rows(lp, 3);
16
17   s4:     lpx_set_row_name(lp, 1, "p");
18   s5:     lpx_set_row_bnds(lp, 1, LPX_UP, 0.0,
         100.0);
19   s6:     lpx_set_row_name(lp, 2, "q");
20   s7:     lpx_set_row_bnds(lp, 2, LPX_UP, 0.0,
         200.0);
21   s8:     lpx_set_row_name(lp, 3, "r");
22   s9:     lpx_set_row_bnds(lp, 3, LPX_UP, 0.0,
         300.0);
23
24   s10:    lpx_add_cols(lp, 3);
25
26   s11:    lpx_set_col_name(lp, 1, "x1");
27   s12:    lpx_set_col_bnds(lp, 1, LPX_LO, 0.0,
         0.0);
28   s13:    lpx_set_col_name(lp, 2, "x2");
29   s14:    lpx_set_col_bnds(lp, 2, LPX_LO, 0.0,
         0.0);
30   s15:    lpx_set_col_name(lp, 3, "x3");
31   s16:    lpx_set_col_bnds(lp, 3, LPX_LO, 0.0,
         0.0);
32
33   s17:    rn[1] = 1, cn[1] = 1, a[1] =  1.0;
34   s18:    rn[2] = 1, cn[2] = 2, a[2] =  1.0;
35   s19:    rn[3] = 1, cn[3] = 3, a[3] =  1.0;
36   s20:    rn[4] = 2, cn[4] = 1, a[4] = 10.0;
37   s21:    rn[5] = 3, cn[5] = 1, a[5] =  2.0;
38   s22:    rn[6] = 2, cn[6] = 2, a[6] =  4.0;
39   s23:    rn[7] = 3, cn[7] = 2, a[7] =  2.0;
40   s24:    rn[8] = 2, cn[8] = 3, a[8] =  5.0;
41   s25:    rn[9] = 3, cn[9] = 3, a[9] =  6.0;
42   s26:    lpx_load_mat3(lp, 9, rn, cn, a);
43
```

```
44  s27:  lpx_set_obj_dir(lp, LPX_MAX);
45
46  s28:  lpx_set_col_coef(lp, 1, 10.0);
47  s29:  lpx_set_col_coef(lp, 2, 6.0);
48  s30:  lpx_set_col_coef(lp, 3, 4.0);
49
50  s31:  lpx_simplex(lp);
51
52  s32:  Z = lpx_get_obj_val(lp);
53  s33:  lpx_get_col_info(lp, 1, NULL, &x1,
      NULL);
54  s34:  lpx_get_col_info(lp, 2, NULL, &x2,
      NULL);
55  s35:  lpx_get_col_info(lp, 3, NULL, &x3,
      NULL);
56
57  s36:  printf("\nZ = %g; x1 = %g; x2 = %g; x3
      = %g\n", Z, x1, x2, x3);
58
59  s37:  lpx_delete_prob(lp);
60
61        return 0;
62  }
63
64  /* eof */
```

Code Fragment 63: Using GLPK API (C example).

Because of the argument handling changes that will be implemented for the PHP extension to GLPK, the equivalent PHP code for the above example is much smaller. The PHP equivalent of Code Fragment 63 is shown below.

```
1   <?php
2     $prob = new GLPKProblem( "sample", 3, 3,
      LPX_MAX );
3
4     $prob->SetRowNames( array( 'p', 'q', 'r' )
      );
5     $prob->SetColNames( array( 'x', 'y', 'x' )
      );
6
7     $prob->SetRowBound( 1, LPX_UP, 100.0 );
8     $prob->SetRowBound( 2, LPX_UP, 600.0 );
9     $prob->SetRowBound( 3, LPX_UP, 300.0 );
10
11    $prob->SetColBound( 1, LPX_LO, 0,0 );
12    $prob->SetColBound( 2, LPX_LO, 0,0 );
13    $prob->SetColBound( 3, LPX_LO, 0,0 );
```

```
14
15    $prob->SetObjCoeffs( array( 10, 6, 4 ) );
16
17    $prob->SetMatrix( array( 1, 1, 1,
18                            10, 4, 5,
19                             2, 2, 6  ) );
20
21    $result = $prob->Solve();
22
23    foreach ( $result->cols as $col )
24    {
25      print( $col->name . ' = ' . $col->primal
    . "\n" );
26    }
27
28    print( "Objective value: " . $result-
    >objective . "\n" );
29
30    //var_dump( $result );
31
32    $prob->Delete();
33  ?>
```

Code Fragment 64: PHP equivalent to Code Fragment 63.

The first section of code to highlight in the implementation of this extension is in the header file, *php_glpk.h*.

```
1   ZEND_BEGIN_MODULE_GLOBALS(glpk)
2          long    messagelevel;
3          long    scale;
4          long    dual;
5          long    price;
6          double  relax;
7          long    round;
8          long    iters_limit;
9          long    iters_count;
10         double  time_limit;
11         long    output_freq;
12         double  output_delay;
13         long    mip_branch_heuristic;
14         long    mip_backtrack_heuristic;
15         long    presolve;
16  ZEND_END_MODULE_GLOBALS(glpk)
17
18  typedef struct _glpk_resource
19  {
20    LPX* lp;
21  } glpk_resource;
22
```

```
23  #define le_glpk_name "GLPK Resource"
```

Code Fragment 65: Relevant changes to the php_glpk.h header file.

The first 16 lines define the global variables used by this extension. Each of the globals is mapped to an INI file value, so that the general parameters to the problem object can be set globally as needed for the problem set. The internal GLPK object can be *tuned* using these parameters. Since this is very specific to GLPK, there is no full documentation of these settings here. Suffice it to say that these internal parameters affect the performance and configuration of the solver and are therefore excellent examples of the types of parameters that should be exposed via the PHP INI file.

Lines 18 through 23 define the resource type and name used by the GLPK extension. The resource is simply a structure containing a pointer to an LPX structure which is defined internally by the GLPK engine. This object pointer is used by every GLPK function.

The next section of code to consider is the implementation file itself. Not all of the code in the sample is shown in this document as there are over 1,300 lines. Rather, the code will be shown and described in sections below.

The first section (below) shows the function entries for the procedural functions and also the methods available via the exposed object.

```
1   /* {{{ glpk_functions[]
2    *
```

```
3    * Every user visible function must have an
     entry in glpk_functions[].
4    */
5    function_entry glpk_functions[] = {
6        PHP_FE(confirm_glpk_compiled,   NULL)
     /* For testing, remove later. */
7        PHP_FE(glpk_create, NULL)
8        PHP_FE(glpk_set_row_names,   NULL)
9        PHP_FE(glpk_set_col_names,   NULL)
10       PHP_FE(glpk_set_row_bound,   NULL)
11       PHP_FE(glpk_set_col_bound,   NULL)
12       PHP_FE(glpk_set_matrix, NULL)
13       PHP_FE(glpk_set_obj_coeffs, NULL)
14       PHP_FE(glpk_solve,   NULL)
15       PHP_FE(glpk_get_objective,   NULL)
16       PHP_FE(glpk_get_col_info,    NULL)
17       PHP_FE(glpk_delete, NULL)
18       PHP_FE(glpk_get_row_info,    NULL)
19       PHP_FE(glpk_set_coltypes,    NULL)
20       PHP_FE(glpk_load,    NULL)
21       PHP_FE(glpk_store,   NULL)
     {NULL, NULL, NULL}  /* Must be the last line
     in glpk_functions[] */
22   };
     /* }}} */
23
24   function_entry glpkproblem_functions[] = {
25     PHP_FALIAS( glpkproblem, glpk_create, NULL
     )
26     PHP_FALIAS( setrownames,
     glpk_set_row_names, NULL )
27     PHP_FALIAS( setcolnames,
     glpk_set_col_names, NULL )
28     PHP_FALIAS( setrowbound,
     glpk_set_row_bound, NULL )
29     PHP_FALIAS( setcolbound,
     glpk_set_col_bound, NULL )
30     PHP_FALIAS( setmatrix,   glpk_set_matrix,
     NULL )
31     PHP_FALIAS( setobjcoeffs,
     glpk_set_obj_coeffs, NULL )
32     PHP_FALIAS( solve, glpk_solve, NULL )
33     PHP_FALIAS( delete, glpk_delete, NULL )
34     PHP_FALIAS( setcoltypes,
     glpk_set_coltypes, NULL )
35     {NULL, NULL, NULL}    /* Must be the last
     line in glpk_functions[] */
36   };
```

Code Fragment 66: Function and method entries for GLPK extension.

The main entry of note is line 25 which sets up the constructor of the GLPKProblem class as a reference to the **glpk_create()** function.

Next, the following section of code shows the INI file and globals setup. It is important to remember that it is your responsibility to set the default values for your extension. This is because there may be no *php.ini* file or the values relating to your extension may not be present therein.

```
1   /* {{{ PHP_INI
2    */
3   PHP_INI_BEGIN()
4       STD_PHP_INI_ENTRY("glpk.messagelevel",
    "0", PHP_INI_ALL, OnUpdateInt, messagelevel,
    zend_glpk_globals, glpk_globals)
5       STD_PHP_INI_ENTRY("glpk.scale", "3",
    PHP_INI_ALL, OnUpdateInt, scale,
    zend_glpk_globals, glpk_globals)
6       STD_PHP_INI_ENTRY("glpk.dual", "0",
    PHP_INI_ALL, OnUpdateInt, dual,
    zend_glpk_globals, glpk_globals)
7       STD_PHP_INI_ENTRY("glpk.price", "1",
    PHP_INI_ALL, OnUpdateInt, price,
    zend_glpk_globals, glpk_globals)
8       STD_PHP_INI_ENTRY("glpk.relax", "0.07",
    PHP_INI_ALL, OnUpdateReal, relax,
    zend_glpk_globals, glpk_globals)
9       STD_PHP_INI_ENTRY("glpk.round", "0",
    PHP_INI_ALL, OnUpdateInt, round,
    zend_glpk_globals, glpk_globals)
10      STD_PHP_INI_ENTRY("glpk.iters_limit", "-
    1", PHP_INI_ALL, OnUpdateInt, iters_limit,
    zend_glpk_globals, glpk_globals)
11      STD_PHP_INI_ENTRY("glpk.iters_count",
    "0", PHP_INI_ALL, OnUpdateInt, iters_count,
    zend_glpk_globals, glpk_globals)
12      STD_PHP_INI_ENTRY("glpk.time_limit", "-
    1.0", PHP_INI_ALL, OnUpdateReal, time_limit,
    zend_glpk_globals, glpk_globals)
13      STD_PHP_INI_ENTRY("glpk.output_freq",
    "200", PHP_INI_ALL, OnUpdateInt,
    output_freq, zend_glpk_globals,
    glpk_globals)
14      STD_PHP_INI_ENTRY("glpk.output_delay",
    "0.0", PHP_INI_ALL, OnUpdateReal,
    output_delay, zend_glpk_globals,
    glpk_globals)
```

```
15      STD_PHP_INI_ENTRY("glpk.mip_branch_heuristic
        ", "2", PHP_INI_ALL, OnUpdateInt,
        mip_branch_heuristic, zend_glpk_globals,
        glpk_globals)
16      STD_PHP_INI_ENTRY("glpk.mip_backtrack_heuris
        tic", "2", PHP_INI_ALL, OnUpdateInt,
        mip_backtrack_heuristic, zend_glpk_globals,
        glpk_globals)
17          STD_PHP_INI_ENTRY("glpk.presolve", "0",
        PHP_INI_ALL, OnUpdateInt, presolve,
        zend_glpk_globals, glpk_globals)
18      PHP_INI_END()
19      /* }}} */
20
21      /* {{{ php_glpk_init_globals
22       */
23      static void
        php_glpk_init_globals(zend_glpk_globals
        *glpk_globals)
24      {
25          glpk_globals->messagelevel = 0;
26          glpk_globals->scale = 3;
27          glpk_globals->dual = 0;
28          glpk_globals->price = 1;
29          glpk_globals->relax = 0.07;
30          glpk_globals->round = 0;
31          glpk_globals->iters_limit = -1;
32          glpk_globals->iters_count = 0;
33          glpk_globals->time_limit = -1.0;
34          glpk_globals->output_freq  = 200;
35          glpk_globals->output_delay = 0.0;
36          glpk_globals->mip_branch_heuristic = 2;
37          glpk_globals->mip_backtrack_heuristic =
        2;
38          glpk_globals->presolve  0;
39      }
40      /* }}} */
```

Code Fragment 67: INI and globals setup for GLPK extension.

All of the INI entries above use the standard macro along with the standard update handlers (OnUpdateInt and OnUpdateFloat in this extension). As described earlier in this document, using the standard update handlers ensures that the module globals are automatically updated and therefore always synchronized with INI value changes.

The next section of code is the module initialization function.

```
1    PHP_MINIT_FUNCTION(glpk)
2    {
3        zend_class_entry tmp_ce;
4
5        ZEND_INIT_MODULE_GLOBALS(glpk,
     php_glpk_init_globals, NULL);
6        REGISTER_INI_ENTRIES();
7
8        INIT_CLASS_ENTRY( tmp_ce, "glpkproblem",
     glpkproblem_functions );
9        glpkproblem_ce_ptr =
     zend_register_internal_class( &tmp_ce
     TSRMLS_CC );
10
11       // register constants
12       REGISTER_LONG_CONSTANT( "LPX_MIN",
     LPX_MIN, CONST_CS | CONST_PERSISTENT );
13       REGISTER_LONG_CONSTANT( "LPX_MAX",
     LPX_MAX, CONST_CS | CONST_PERSISTENT );
14       REGISTER_LONG_CONSTANT( "LPX_LP",
     LPX_LP,  CONST_CS | CONST_PERSISTENT );
15       REGISTER_LONG_CONSTANT( "LPX_MIP",
     LPX_MIP, CONST_CS | CONST_PERSISTENT );
16
17
18       REGISTER_LONG_CONSTANT( "LPX_FR",
     LPX_FR,  CONST_CS | CONST_PERSISTENT );
19       REGISTER_LONG_CONSTANT( "LPX_LO",
     LPX_LO,  CONST_CS | CONST_PERSISTENT );
20       REGISTER_LONG_CONSTANT( "LPX_UP",
     LPX_UP,  CONST_CS | CONST_PERSISTENT );
21       REGISTER_LONG_CONSTANT( "LPX_DB",
     LPX_DB,  CONST_CS | CONST_PERSISTENT );
22       REGISTER_LONG_CONSTANT( "LPX_FX",
     LPX_FX,  CONST_CS | CONST_PERSISTENT );
23
24       REGISTER_LONG_CONSTANT( "LPX_E_OK",
     LPX_E_OK,    CONST_CS | CONST_PERSISTENT );
25       REGISTER_LONG_CONSTANT( "LPX_E_FAULT",
     LPX_E_FAULT,  CONST_CS | CONST_PERSISTENT );
26       REGISTER_LONG_CONSTANT( "LPX_E_OBJLL",
     LPX_E_OBJLL,  CONST_CS | CONST_PERSISTENT );
27       REGISTER_LONG_CONSTANT( "LPX_E_OBJUL",
     LPX_E_OBJUL,  CONST_CS | CONST_PERSISTENT );
28       REGISTER_LONG_CONSTANT( "LPX_E_ITLIM",
     LPX_E_ITLIM,  CONST_CS | CONST_PERSISTENT );
29       REGISTER_LONG_CONSTANT( "LPX_E_TMLIM",
     LPX_E_TMLIM,  CONST_CS | CONST_PERSISTENT );
```

```
30      REGISTER_LONG_CONSTANT( "LPX_E_SING",
   LPX_E_SING,  CONST_CS | CONST_PERSISTENT );
31      REGISTER_LONG_CONSTANT( "LPX_E_NOPFS",
   LPX_E_NOPFS,  CONST_CS | CONST_PERSISTENT );
32      REGISTER_LONG_CONSTANT( "LPX_E_NODFS",
   LPX_E_NODFS,  CONST_CS | CONST_PERSISTENT );
33
34
35      REGISTER_LONG_CONSTANT( "LPX_OPT",
   LPX_OPT,      CONST_CS | CONST_PERSISTENT );
36      REGISTER_LONG_CONSTANT( "LPX_FEAS",
   LPX_FEAS,     CONST_CS | CONST_PERSISTENT );
37      REGISTER_LONG_CONSTANT( "LPX_INFEAS",
   LPX_INFEAS,  CONST_CS | CONST_PERSISTENT );
38      REGISTER_LONG_CONSTANT( "LPX_NOFEAS",
   LPX_NOFEAS,  CONST_CS | CONST_PERSISTENT );
39      REGISTER_LONG_CONSTANT( "LPX_UNBND",
   LPX_UNBND,    CONST_CS | CONST_PERSISTENT );
40      REGISTER_LONG_CONSTANT( "LPX_UNDEF",
   LPX_UNDEF,    CONST_CS | CONST_PERSISTENT );
41
42      REGISTER_LONG_CONSTANT( "LPX_CV",
   LPX_CV,   CONST_CS | CONST_PERSISTENT );
43      REGISTER_LONG_CONSTANT( "LPX_IV",
   LPX_IV,   CONST_CS | CONST_PERSISTENT );
44
45      // register resources
46      le_glpk =
   zend_register_list_destructors_ex(
   _glpk_destruction_handler, NULL,
   le_glpk_name, module_number );
47
48      // register callback for GLPK errors
49      glp_lib_set_fault_hook( NULL,
   _glpk_fault_hook );
50      glp_lib_set_print_hook( NULL,
   _glpk_fault_hook );
51
52      return SUCCESS;
53  }
```

Code Fragment 68: GLPK module initialization.

Lines 3, 8 and 9 of the module initialization function register the internal class, **GLPKProblem**. Lines 11 through 43 register the named constants for the extension. The resource destruction handler is registered in line 46. Finally, lines 48 through 50 are code specific to this extension. In these lines, error-handling callbacks are registered with the GLPK library. This is done so that the library does not print the error messages to stdout or stderr, but relays the messages through the callback function.

```
1  PHP_MSHUTDOWN_FUNCTION(glpk)
2  {
3      UNREGISTER_INI_ENTRIES();
4
5      glp_lib_set_fault_hook( NULL, NULL );
6      glp_lib_set_print_hook( NULL, NULL );
7
8      return SUCCESS;
9  }
```

Code Fragment 69: GLPK module shutdown.

The GLPK module shutdown function is shown in Code Fragment 69. The main work done here is to reset the error-handling callback functions to NULL which effectively unhooks the GLPK extension from underlying library.

The **glpk_create()** function is the primary function to be examined in this extension. It is important to recall that this extension may be used from a procedural programming perspective or from an object oriented perspective. The difference is important in how the **glpk_create()** function behaves internally. If called directly (procedurally), this function returns a resource handle that must be used in all other extension functions. Otherwise, the **glpk_create()** function handles the **new GLPKProblem(...)** syntax and stores the resource handle internally in the *$this* pointer.

The **glpk_create()** function accepts six parameters, the final three are optional. The parameters are described in the table below.

prob_name	String value used to set the

	external name of the problem.
rows	Integer value representing the number of rows (constraints) in the problem.
cols	Integer value representing the number of columns (structural variables) in the problem.
objective_dir	Integer – either LPX_MIN or LPX_MAX – representing the optimization direction for the problem. The default value is LPX_MIN.
problem_class	Integer – either LPX_LP or LPX_MIP – representing the class of the problem. The default value is LPX_LP.
objective_function_name	External name of the objective function. Defaults to "Objective".

Table 26: Arguments to the glpk_create() function.

The actual implementation of this function is below.

```
1   PHP_FUNCTION(glpk_create)
2   {
3     char *prob_name = NULL;
4     char *objective_function_name = NULL;
5     int argc = ZEND_NUM_ARGS();
6     int prob_name_len;
7     int objective_function_name_len;
8     long rows;
9     long cols;
10    long objective_dir;
11    long problem_class;
12    glpk_resource* resource;
13    int rscid;
14
15    /*
16      call types:
17          glpk_create( string prob_name, int
    rows, int cols,
18                       [int objective_dir,
    [int problem_class,
19                       [string
    objective_function_name]]] )
20          new GLPKProblem( <same arguments> );
21
22      returns:
```

```
23          resource ID or FALSE
24          $this contains resource ID as a
   property or uninitialized $this
25   */
26

   if (zend_parse_parameters(argc TSRMLS_CC,
   "sll|lls", &prob_name, &prob_name_len,
   &rows, &cols, &objective_dir,
   &problem_class, &objective_function_name,
   &objective_function_name_len) == FAILURE)
27   {
28      if ( getThis() == NULL )
29      {
30         // return PHP 'false' if this is a
   procedural call
31         RETURN_FALSE;
32      }
33      else
34      {
35         // simply return if this was a call to
   new GLPKProblem
36         return;
37      }
38   }
39
40   // set default function values as needed
41   switch( argc )
42   {
43     case 3: // objective_dir omitted,
   default = LPX_MIN
44        objective_dir = LPX_MIN;
45        // fall through
46     case 4: // problem_class omitted,
   default = LPX_LP
47        problem_class = LPX_LP;
48        // fall through
49     case 5: // objective function name
   omitted, default = "Objective"
50        objective_function_name = "Objective";
51        // fall through
52   }
53
54   // check all the parameters for
   correctness
55   if ( lpx_check_name( prob_name ) )
56   {
57      // bogus name
58      zend_error( E_ERROR, "Bad problem name,
   '%s', use only [A-Za-z0-9]", prob_name );
59   }
60
61   if ( lpx_check_name(
   objective_function_name ) )
62   {
63      // bogus name
```

```
64      zend_error( E_ERROR, "Bad objective
   function name, '%s', use only [A-Za-z0-9]",
   objective_function_name );
65   }
66
67   if ( rows <= 0 )
68   {
69     // rows must be > 0
70     zend_error( E_ERROR, "Number of rows
   must be > 0" );
71   }
72
73   if ( cols <= 0 )
74   {
75     // cols must be > 0
76     zend_error( E_ERROR, "Number of columns
   must be > 0" );
77   }
78
79   if ( ( objective_dir != LPX_MIN ) && (
   objective_dir != LPX_MAX ) )
80   {
81      zend_error( E_ERROR, "The objective
   direction must be either LPX_MIN or LPX_MAX"
   );
82   }
83
84   if ( ( problem_class != LPX_LP ) && (
   problem_class != LPX_MIP ) )
85   {
86      zend_error( E_ERROR, "The problem class
   must be either LPX_LP or LPX_MIP" );
87   }
88
89   // now allocate the resource container
90   resource = emalloc( sizeof( glpk_resource
   ) );
91
92   // call the GLPK functions to properly
   initialize the new problem
93   resource->lp = lpx_create_prob();
94
95   // set the control parameters of the
   problem based on INI/global values
96   lpx_set_int_parm ( resource->lp,
   LPX_K_MSGLEV, GLPK_G( messagelevel ) );
97   lpx_set_int_parm ( resource->lp,
   LPX_K_SCALE,  GLPK_G( scale      ) );
98   lpx_set_int_parm ( resource->lp,
   LPX_K_DUAL,   GLPK_G( dual       ) );
99   lpx_set_int_parm ( resource->lp,
   LPX_K_PRICE,  GLPK_G( price      ) );
100  lpx_set_int_parm ( resource->lp,
   LPX_K_ROUND,  GLPK_G( round      ) );
```

```
101   lpx_set_int_parm ( resource->lp,
   LPX_K_ITLIM,  GLPK_G( iters_limit  ) );
102   lpx_set_int_parm ( resource->lp,
   LPX_K_ITCNT,  GLPK_G( iters_count  ) );
103   lpx_set_int_parm ( resource->lp,
   LPX_K_OUTFRQ, GLPK_G( output_freq  ) );
104   lpx_set_int_parm ( resource->lp,
   LPX_K_BRANCH, GLPK_G( mip_branch_heuristic )
   );
105   lpx_set_int_parm ( resource->lp,
   LPX_K_BTRACK, GLPK_G(
   mip_backtrack_heuristic ) );
106   lpx_set_int_parm ( resource->lp,
   LPX_K_PRESOL, GLPK_G( presolve    ) );
107   lpx_set_real_parm( resource->lp,
   LPX_K_RELAX,  GLPK_G( relax       ) );
108   lpx_set_real_parm( resource->lp,
   LPX_K_TMLIM,  GLPK_G( time_limit  ) );
109   lpx_set_real_parm( resource->lp,
   LPX_K_OUTDLY, GLPK_G( output_delay ) );
110
111   // set up the problem
112   lpx_add_rows     ( resource->lp, rows );
113   lpx_add_cols     ( resource->lp, cols );
114   lpx_set_prob_name( resource->lp, prob_name
   );
115   lpx_set_obj_name ( resource->lp,
   objective_function_name );
116   lpx_set_obj_dir  ( resource->lp,
   objective_dir );
117   lpx_set_class    ( resource->lp,
   problem_class );
118
119   rscid = ZEND_REGISTER_RESOURCE( NULL,
   resource, le_glpk );
120
121   if ( getThis() )
122   {
123     // we're in a new GLPKProblem() call,
   return through $this
124     object_init_ex( getThis(),
   glpkproblem_ce_ptr );
125     add_property_resource( getThis(),
   "rscid", rscid );
126   }
127   else
128   {
129     // we're in procedural call, return the
   resource directly
130     RETVAL_RESOURCE( rscid );
131   }
132 }
```

**Code Fragment 70: Implementation of the glpk_create()
function.**

This function is doubtless the largest single function illustrated in this document. Line 26 is the first relevant line of code in this function. This is the argument parsing function call as illustrated in several other examples. No matter the calling type, procedural or object oriented, the incoming argument list is identical. If the argument list is invalid, this function returns to the caller.

Lines 40 through 52 set the optional parameters to their default values if needed. Lines 54 through 87 check all the input arguments for valid values. For names used internally, the **lpx_check_name()** function is used. Other arguments are checked for valid values or ranges.

> Note that all of the primary GLPK API functions are prefixed with **lpx_**.

Assuming all the arguments are valid, the next block of code (lines 89 through 93) allocate a resource container and then initialize the problem object within the container.

Lines 95 through 109 set the problem control parameters based on the module INI/global values. Lines 111 through 117 then set the intial values of the problem including the number of constraints and variables, the name of the problem, the objective direction and problem class.

In line 119, the resource is registered with the Zend engine so that it gets destructed properly. Finally in lines 121 through 132, the resource is returned to the caller. If the result of the **getThis()** function is not

NULL (line 121), then the newly allocated resource is added as a property to the *$this* variable (lines 123 through 125). Otherwise, the resource is simply returned to the caller verbatim (line 130).

The next function to be discussed is the **glpk_set_row_names()** function. This function will be described in detail as it is the template for several of the extension functions. In fact, most of the remaining functions work in exactly the same way.

```
1   PHP_FUNCTION(glpk_set_row_names)
2   {
3     int              argc = ZEND_NUM_ARGS();
4     zval***          arg_array;
5     zval**           tmp;
6     glpk_resource*   resource;
7
8     /*
9       call types:
10            glpk_set_row_names( resource
      problem, array names );
11            GLPKProblem->SetRowNames( array
      names );
12
13        returns:
14            no return value
15     */
16     arg_array = emalloc( sizeof( zval** ) *
      argc );
17     if ( zend_get_parameters_array_ex( argc,
      arg_array ) != SUCCESS )
18     {
19       zend_error( E_ERROR, "Internal Error:
      Problem retrieving arguments" );
20     }
21
22     resource = _glpk_get_resource( getThis(),
      arg_array );
23     if ( !resource )
24     {
25       zend_error( E_ERROR, "Internal Error:
      Problem retrieving resource" );
26     }
27
28     if ( getThis() )
29     {
30       // check that there is at least one
      argument
31       _glpk_assert_argc_ge( argc, 1 );
```

```
32       _glpk_set_row_names( resource,
    arg_array[0] );
33    }
34    else
35    {
36       // check that there are at least two
    arguments
37       _glpk_assert_argc_ge( argc, 2 );
38       _glpk_set_row_names( resource,
    arg_array[1] );
39    }
40
41    efree( arg_array );
42  }
```

**Code Fragment 71: Implementation of
glpk_set_row_names function.**

The general concept of this function is to first retrieve
the arguments into a zval array, then determine the
type of call (procedural or object_oriented) and finally
pass the arguments to an internal worker function.
Line 16 allocates the zval array using the **emalloc()**
function and the number of arguments passed into
the function. Line 22 uses an internal function to
retrieve the **glpk_resource** pointer from either the
$this variable or the first argument. The internal
functions **_glpk_assert_argc_ge()** and
_glpk_get_resource() are shown in Code Fragment
72 andCode Fragment 73, respectively.

Once the resource pointer is obtained, the internal
version of this function, **_glpk_set_row_names()** is
called. If the call is procedural, the internal function
is called on line 38, passing the resource pointer and
the second argument to the function (the array of
names). If the call is object oriented, the internal
function is called on line 32, passing the resource
pointer and the first argument to the method.

Using this methodology for all internal functions
simplifies the development of a co-existing procedural

and object-oriented implementation. The internal functions to ensure the proper number of arguments and to retrieve the internal resource pointer are shown below.

```
1   void _glpk_assert_argc_ge( int argc, int
    argc_reqd )
2   {
3     if ( argc < argc_reqd )
4     {
5       zend_error( E_ERROR, "Not enough
    parameters" );
6     }
7   }
```

**Code Fragment 72: Implementation of the
_glpk_assert_argc_ge function.**

```
1   glpk_resource*  _glpk_get_resource( zval*
    this_ptr, zval** arg_array[] )
2   {
3     zval**          tmp;
4     glpk_resource*   resource = NULL;
5     TSRMLS_FETCH();
6     /*
7       The ZEND_FETCH_RESOURCE cannot be used
    in the context of this function
8       because part of the macro expects the
    'return_value' variable to be
9       available.
10    */
11
12    if ( this_ptr )
13    {
14      // OO call, get glpk_resource* from
    $this
15      if ( SUCCESS == zend_hash_find(
    Z_OBJPROP_P( this_ptr ), "rscid", sizeof(
    "rscid" ), (void**) &tmp ) )
      {
16        //ZEND_FETCH_RESOURCE( resource,
    glpk_resource *, tmp, -1, le_glpk_name,
    le_glpk );
17        resource = (glpk_resource *)
    zend_fetch_resource( tmp TSRMLS_CC, -1,
    le_glpk_name, NULL, 1, le_glpk );
      }
18    }
19    else
20    {
```

```
21        // ensure that first parameter is a
    resource
22        if ( Z_TYPE_PP( arg_array[0] ) !=
    IS_RESOURCE )
23        {
24            zend_error( E_ERROR, "First argument
        must be a valid %s resource ID",
        le_glpk_name );
25        }
26
27        // ensure that first parameter is a
    resource of the correct type
28        if ( strcmp(
    zend_rsrc_list_get_rsrc_type( Z_RESVAL_PP(
    arg_array[0] ) TSRMLS_CC ), le_glpk_name ) )
29        {
30            zend_error( E_ERROR, "First argument
        must be a valid %s resource ID",
        le_glpk_name );
31        }
32
33        // procedural call, get glpk_resoure*
    from first param
34        //ZEND_FETCH_RESOURCE( resource,
        glpk_resource *, arg_array[0], -1,
        le_glpk_name, le_glpk );
35        resource = (glpk_resource *)
        zend_fetch_resource( arg_array[0] TSRMLS_CC,
        -1, le_glpk_name, NULL, 1, le_glpk );
        }
36
37    return resource;
38 }
```

**Code Fragment 73: Implementation of the
_glpk_get_resource function.**

The **_glpk_assert_argc_ge()** function is extremely
simple and should require no explanation. However,
the **_glpk_get_resource()** function is relatively
complex and requires some explanation. The purpose
of the function is to return a **gplk_resource** pointer
from either the *$this* variable or the passed resource
handle. Lines 12 through 18 deal with the case that
the resource is stored in the *$this* pointer. In this
extension, I assume that the *$this* >*rscid* member is not
used for any reason by the end programmer.
Therefore, the implementation simply locates the

object's *rscid* member using the **zend_hash_find()** function then uses the **zend_fetch_resource()** function to retrieve the resource pointer from the zval.

If this is not an object-oriented call, then the resource handle is expected to be the first element of the argument array. Lines 22 through 25 check to ensure that that argument is actually a resource type argument. Lines 28 through 31 then check that the resource is the right type, using the **zend_rsrc_list_get_rsrc_type()** function. This function accepts a resource id and returns a C string (character pointer), the resource type. Finally the resource is retrieved from the zval and the resource pointer is returned.

It should be noted that (as the comments in lines 6 through 10 state) the **ZEND_FETCH_RESOUCE** macro cannot be used in the context of this function. That is due to the fact that the macro expects to have a variable called *return_value* locally available. A note regarding this is included in the section Working with Resources which starts on page 91.

Returning to the **glpk_set_row_names()** function, the last part of the function is to call the internal code that actually does the work. The implementation of that internal function is **_glpk_set_row_names()** and is shown below.

```
1    void _glpk_set_row_names( glpk_resource*
     resource, zval** names )
2    {
3        char*      tmpname;
4        int        index;
5        int        num_items;
6        zval**     item;
7
8        if ( Z_TYPE_PP( names ) != IS_ARRAY )
```

```
9     {
10       zend_error( E_ERROR, "The 'names'
      parameter must be an array" );
11     }
12
13     num_items = zend_hash_num_elements(
      Z_ARRVAL_PP( names ) );
14     if ( num_items != lpx_get_num_rows(
      resource->lp ) )
15     {
16       zend_error( E_ERROR, "Number of row
      names must be equal to number of rows in
      problem (%d)",
17                      lpx_get_num_rows( resource-
      >lp ) );
18     }
19
20     zend_hash_internal_pointer_reset(
      Z_ARRVAL_PP( names ) );
21     for ( index = 0; index < num_items;
      index++ )
22     {
23       zend_hash_get_current_data( Z_ARRVAL_PP(
      names ), (void**) &item );
24       convert_to_string_ex( item );
25       tmpname = Z_STRVAL_PP( item );
26
27       if ( lpx_check_name( tmpname ) )
28       {
29         zend_error( E_ERROR, "Row name, '%s',
      is invalid", tmpname );
30       }
31       else
32       {
33         lpx_set_row_name( resource->lp, index
      + 1, tmpname );
34       }
35
36       zend_hash_move_forward( Z_ARRVAL_PP(
      names ) );
37     }
38   }
```

**Code Fragment 74: Implementation of the
_glpk_set_row_names function.**

The purpose of this function is to assign human-readable names to each row in the GLPK problem. In my implementation, the names are assigned via an array of strings. Therefore, this function is mostly an array traversal function that calls an internal GLPK

API function. Lines 8 through 11 ensure that the first
argument passed into the function is an array. Then
the number of elements is retrieved (line 13) and
checked against the number of rows in the problem
(lines 14 through 18). Next, the array is traversed and
each element of the array is checked to ensure the
name is valid to the GLPK engine (line 27). If the
name is valid, it is assigned to the problem in line 33.

> NOTE: The GLPK engine arrays are indexed
> starting from 1, not 0. Therefore all calls to the
> engine referencing arrays or indexes must be
> called accordingly.

The **glpk_set_col_names()**,
glpk_set_row_bound(), **glpk_set_col_bound()**,
glpk_set_matrix(), **glpk_set_obj_coeffs()** and
glpk_set_coltypes() functions are all implemented in
exactly the same fashion as the glpk_set_row_names()
function. The only differences are the internal
functions used for each. Since all of these functions
are conceptually the same, they will not be discussed
in this document.

The last two functions that will be documented are
the **glpk_solve()** and **glpk_delete()** functions. The
former is the embodiment of the purpose of the
solver. The latter is a simple resource deletion
function. The implementation of **glpk_solve()** is
shown below.

```
1    PHP_FUNCTION(glpk_solve)
2    {
3        int          argc = ZEND_NUM_ARGS();
4        int          result;
5        zval***      arg_array;
6        zval*        tmp;
7        zval*        rows;
8        zval*        cols;
```

```
9    glpk_resource*      resource;
10   int                 status;
11   int                 index;
12   char*               name;
13   int                 tagx;
14   double              vx, dx;
15   double              objective;
16
17   /*
18     call types:
19         glpk_solve( resource problem );
20         GLPKProblem->Solve( void );
21
22     returns:
23         no return value
24   */
25   arg_array = emalloc( sizeof( zval** ) *
     argc );
26   if ( zend_get_parameters_array_ex( argc,
     arg_array ) != SUCCESS )
27   {
28     zend_error( E_ERROR, "Internal Error:
     Problem retrieving arguments" );
29   }
30
31
32   resource = _glpk_get_resource( getThis(),
     arg_array );
33   if ( !resource )
34   {
35     zend_error( E_ERROR, "Internal Error:
     Problem retrieving resource" );
36   }
37
38   MAKE_STD_ZVAL( rows );
39   MAKE_STD_ZVAL( cols );
40
41   if ( lpx_get_class( resource->lp ) ==
     LPX_LP )
42   {
43     result    = lpx_simplex    ( resource-
     >lp );
44     status    = lpx_get_status ( resource-
     >lp );
45     objective = lpx_get_obj_val( resource-
     >lp );
46   }
47   else
48   {
49     result    = lpx_simplex    ( resource-
     >lp );
50     result    = lpx_integer    ( resource-
     >lp );
51     status    = lpx_get_mip_stat( resource-
     >lp );
```

```
52      objective = lpx_get_mip_obj ( resource-
   >lp );
53    }
54
55    array_init( rows );
56    array_init( cols );
57
58    for ( index = 0; index < lpx_get_num_rows(
   resource->lp ); index++ )
59    {
60      MAKE_STD_ZVAL( tmp );
61      object_init( tmp );
62
63      if ( lpx_get_class( resource->lp ) ==
   LPX_LP )
64        {
65          lpx_get_row_info( resource->lp, index
   + 1, &tagx, &vx, &dx );
66          add_property_double( tmp, "primal", vx
   );
67          add_property_double( tmp, "dual", dx
   );
68          add_property_long  ( tmp, "status",
   tagx );
69        }
70      else
71        {
72          vx = lpx_get_mip_row( resource->lp,
   index + 1 );
73          add_property_double( tmp, "primal", vx
   );
74        }
75
76      name = lpx_get_row_name( resource->lp,
   index + 1 );
77      add_property_string( tmp, "name", name,
   1 );
78
79      add_index_zval( rows, index + 1, tmp );
80    }
81
82    for ( index = 0; index < lpx_get_num_cols(
   resource->lp ); index++ )
83    {
84      MAKE_STD_ZVAL( tmp );
85      object_init( tmp );
86
87      if ( lpx_get_class( resource->lp ) ==
   LPX_LP )
88        {
89          lpx_get_col_info( resource->lp, index
   + 1, &tagx, &vx, &dx );
90          add_property_double( tmp, "primal", vx
   );
```

```
91         add_property_double( tmp, "dual", dx
    );
92         add_property_long  ( tmp, "status",
    tagx );
93       }
94     else
95     {
96         vx = lpx_get_mip_col( resource->lp,
    index + 1 );
97         add_property_double( tmp, "primal", vx
    );
98     }
99
100    name = lpx_get_col_name( resource->lp,
    index + 1 );
101     add_property_string( tmp, "name", name,
    1 );
102
103    add_index_zval( cols, index + 1, tmp );
104    }
105
106  object_init( return_value );
107  add_property_long( return_value, "result",
    result );
108  add_property_long( return_value, "status",
    status );
109  add_property_zval( return_value, "rows",
    rows );
110  add_property_zval( return_value, "cols",
    cols );
111
112  add_property_double( return_value,
    "objective", objective );
113 }
```

Code Fragment 75: Implementation of the glpk_solve function.

The **glpk_solve()** function is the primary function of this extension. It returns an object – a plain PHP object, not an internally-registered class – that consists of the data elements shown in the following table.

result	The internal result code returned from calling the internal solve function.
status	The internal status code returned from calling the internal status function.

cols	An array of objects representing the column solution variables. Each column object contains three data elements, the primal solution, dual solution and status, named **primal**, **dual** and **status**, respectively.
rows	An array of objects representing the row solution variables. Each row object contains three data elements, the primal solution, dual solution and status, named **primal**, **dual** and **status**, respectively.
objective	The objective function value.

The first 36 lines of this function are the same as most of the other functions in this extension – they serve to retrieve the resource pointer for the problem. Lines 38, 39 and 55, 56 allocate and initialize the **rows** and **cols** variables that will be part of the return object. Lines 41 through 53 actually call the solver taking into consideration whether the problem is LP or MIP. Lines 58 through 80 add the row objects to the rows array and lines 82 through 104 add the column objects to the cols array. Finally, in lines 106 through 112, the return value's properties are set and the function ends.

While this is a rather large function, there is nothing that is new except for the calls to the GLPK API functions. Everything else has been discussed in great detail elsewhere in this document.

```
1   PHP_FUNCTION(glpk_delete)
2   {
3     zval**              tmp;
4
5     if ( getThis() )
6     {
7       // OO call, get glpk_resource* from
        $this
8       if ( SUCCESS == zend_hash_find(
        Z_OBJPROP_P( getThis() ), "rscid", sizeof(
        "rscid" ), (void**) &tmp ) )
```

```
9      {
10         zend_list_delete( Z_RESVAL_PP( tmp )
   );
11      }
12    }
13    else
14    {
15      if ( zend_get_parameters_ex( 1, &tmp )
   != SUCCESS )
16      {
17         zend_error( E_ERROR, "First argument
   must be a valid %s resource ID",
   le_glpk_name );
18      }
19
20      // ensure that first parameter is a
   resource
21      if ( Z_TYPE_PP( tmp ) != IS_RESOURCE )
22      {
23         zend_error( E_ERROR, "First argument
   must be a valid %s resource ID",
   le_glpk_name );
24      }
25
26      // ensure that first parameter is a
   resource of the correct type
27      if ( strcmp(
   zend_rsrc_list_get_rsrc_type( Z_RESVAL_PP(
   tmp ) TSRMLC_CC ), le_glpk_name ) )
28      {
29         zend_error( E_ERROR, "First argument
   must be a valid %s resource ID",
   le_glpk_name );
30      }
31
32      zend_list_delete( Z_RESVAL_PP( tmp ) );
33    }
34 }
```

Code Fragment 76: Implementation of the glpk_delete function.

The **glpk_delete()** function is almost identical to the **_glpk_get_resource()** function, but instead of returning a resource pointer, the resource is deleted from the internal list of resources (line 32). This function mirrors the example shown in Code Fragment 41 to de-allocate a resource zval.

GLPK Extension: Summary

Obviously not all of the extension code was explained in this example, but the relevant sections were included and explained in detail. Again, the purpose of the example was to provide a complete real-word example of how to implement an extension in PHP, not to provide a detailed explanation of the GLPK library itself. All of the source code for this example is available for download at http://www.php4devguide.com/.

Self-Contained Extensions

One method of redistribution of extensions is to create a self-contained extension. This process is described briefly in the file README.SELF-CONTAINED-EXTENSIONS in the root directory of the PHP source. The idea is to make it possible for your extension to be build as a stand alone shared library that can then be included into PHP using the *extension* parameter in the *php.ini* file.

To do this, you must use the *phpize* script that is created when you build PHP. Obviously this implies that you have already successfully built PHP. After having done so, change to the extension directory and run the *phpize* script. For example, to make the GLPK extension a stand-alone extension, I created a new directory called *glpk_redist* and copied all of the GLPK source into it. Briefly:

1. cp –rup /path/to/extension/* /path/to/redist
2. phpize

3. aclocal
4. ./configure --with-glpk=shared --with-php-config=/path/to/php-config
5. *edit Makefile*
6. make
7. make install
8. *edit php.ini – add extension=glpk.so*
9. restart web server

The *phpize* and *php config* scripts are found in the PHP bin directory. So, for example, if you built PHP with *prefix=/php*, then the scripts will be found in */php/bin*. Step 3 above may not be necessary, but if you receive a warning message indicating that you should run *aclocal*, do it.

Once steps 1 through 3 are complete, your extension will be almost ready for building. The *phpize* script creates a standard *configure* script in the directory which is used in step 4. The only two arguments to the *configure* script should be the --with-extension (or --enable-extension) argument and the --with-php-config argument as shown above.

In my experience, I found that I had to edit the automatically-generated Makefile. The problem is that there are several references to *libtool* in the Makefile and the reference is to a version of *libtool* that is in the PHP source directory. It may be the case that my installation is faulty, so I edit the Makefile and change the value of the LIBTOOL variable inside the Makefile from its default value to the following:

```
1   LIBTOOL = $(SHELL) /usr/local/bin/libtool
```

This is the full path to my systems default instance of the *libtool* script.

Steps 6 and 7 above build and install the new extension. In this case, the output is a file called *glpk.so* which can be included dynamically into PHP by editing the *php.ini* file.

Using the above method, it becomes possible to create an extension that can be easily redistributed for use in other PHP installations. Note, however, that the *.so* file is not necessarily usable with different versions of PHP. For example, the *glpk.so* file does not work with PHP 5 (beta). The idea for extension redistribution is not to redistribute binaries, but simplify the redistribution of source or to create dynamically loadable extensions to use on your server.

Building Extensions for Windows

The PHP model on Windows is just a little bit different from the PHP model on the unix flavors. Most notably, almost all extensions are loaded dynamically under Windows via standard Windows DLLs (dynamically linked libraries). While it is possible to load extensions dynamically under Linux (as demonstrated in the previous section), many times all of the extensions are build right into the PHP library directly.

If you plan to distribute your extension generally, and you wish to include Windows PHP developers, you'll need to build the DLL for your extension for your users. This is due primarily to the fact that very few developers build PHP on Windows and it's not nearly as straightforward as building PHP on a unix.

Building PHP on Windows

To get started, you must be able to build PHP on Windows in general. This can be done using Microsoft Visual C++. Besides just having the PHP source code, several more files are required to build PHP on Windows. The following table lists these files and their download locations.

PHP Source Code	http://www.php.net/
Cygwin Tools	http://sources.redhat.com/cygwin/
PHP Win32 Build Tools	http://www.php.net/extra/win32build.zip
BCMath (Number) Support	http://www.php.net/extra/number4.tar.gz
Replacement resolve.lib Build Files	http://www.php.net/extra/bindlib_w32.zip

Table 27: Downloads for builing PHP on Windows.

To start, install the Cygwin utilities. You will need to manually add the CYGWIN environment variable to your system after installation. To do this on Windows XP, right click on the *My Computer* icon and select **Properties**. Then, on the **Advanced** tab, click the **Environment Variables** button. Under the **System Variables** section, click the **New** button and enter the variable name (CYGWIN) and the value which is the path to the Cygwin installation (*c:\cygwin* by default). See Figure 1 for an example.

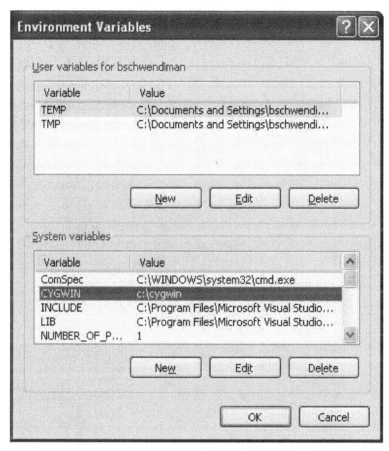

Figure 1: Setting the Cygwin environment variable.

Next, unzip the *win32build.zip* files into a new
directory. Launch Visual C++ and using the **Tools**
menu, select **Options**. Select the directories tab, then
select the option *Executable files* from the drop-down
list labeled *Show directories for*. Add the location of the
Cygwin *bin* directory into this list (see Figure 2).
Next, select *Include files* from the drop-down list and
add the location of the *win32build/include* directory
(see Figure 3). Finally, select *Library files* and add the
location of the *win32build/lib* directory (see Figure 4).

These steps set up the Visual C++ environment to use the additional headers and libraries included in *win32build.zip*.

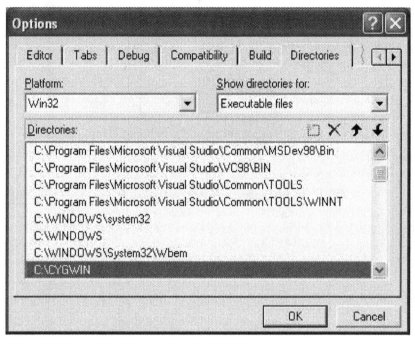

Figure 2: Executable files settings for VC++.

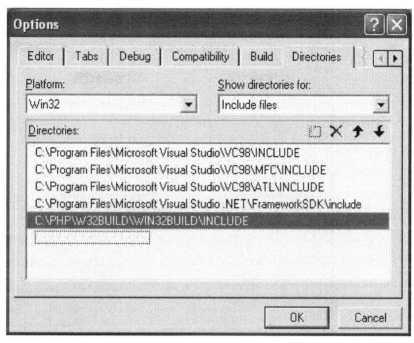

Figure 3: Include files settings for VC++.

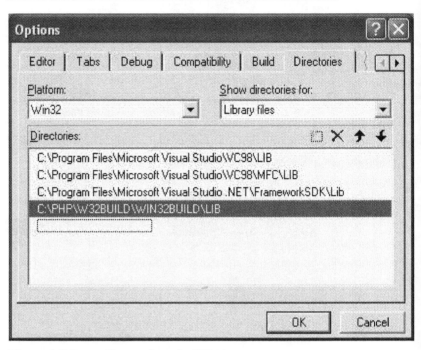

Figure 4: Library files settings for VC++.

Next, unpack the PHP source code and the *number.tar.gz* file. Copy the unpacked files *number.c* and *number.h* (unpacked from *number.tar.gz*) into the *ext/bcmath* directory of the PHP source tree.

Assuming you have done all of the above exactly as described, you are now ready to build PHP for Windows. Start Visual C++ and open the *php4ts.dsp* project file found in the *win32* directory of the PHP source. This project contains several build configurations. The best build configuration to get started is the CLI executable version of PHP. To select this build configuration, select the **Set active configuration** menu item from the **Build** menu. Then choose the *php4ts_cli – Win32_Release_TS* option (see Figure 5).

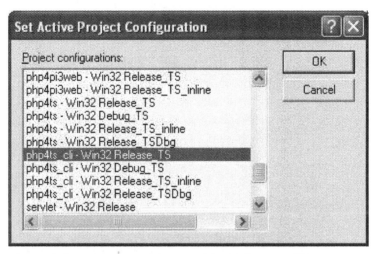

Figure 5: Selecting the php4ts_cli – Win32_Release_TS build configuration.

Next select **Build php.exe** from the **Build** menu or press the **F7** button to build PHP. If all goes well, you have a custom-built PHP executable available for use. As part of the build process, the *php4ts.dll* is also built. This DLL is required by the *php.exe* binary, so it must be copied into the DLL search path or into the same directory as *php.exe*.

Building a PHP Extension on Windows

After successfully building PHP on Windows, you can now begin the process of building your custom extension. Remember, the goal of this is to create a DLL file that can be dynamically loaded by PHP at runtime.

The quickest method for accomplishing this is to move your existing extension into the PHP source tree and then build the extension as a separate Visual C++ project. To do this, you will need a version of *php.exe* on the Windows machine and you will need Cygwin.

The first step is to create the Visual C++ project (.dsp) file. This is accomplished using the *ext_skel _win32.php* script in the *ext* directory of the PHP source. If you have already build your extension on a unix system, then you will need to make a small modification to the *ext_skel_win32.php* script before running it. The code for the script is shown below.

```php
1   <?php
2   /* $Id: ext_skel_win32.php,v 1.1.2.1
    2003/01/31 18:50:41 fmk Exp $ */
3
4   if (php_sapi_name() != "cli") {
5           echo "Please run this script using
    the CLI version of PHP\n";
6           exit;
7   }
8   /*
9           This script can be used on Win32
    systems
10
11          1) Make sure you have CygWin
    installed
12          2) Adjust the $cygwin_path to match
    your installation
13          3) Change the environment cariable
    PATHEXT to include .PHP
14          4) run ext_skel --ext_name=...
15                  the first time you run this
    script you will be asked to
16                  associate it with a program.
    chooses the CLI version of php.
17  */
18
19  $cygwin_path = 'c:\cygwin\bin';
20
21  $path = getenv("PATH");
22  putenv("PATH=$cygwin_path;$path");
23
24  array_shift($argv);
```

```php
25  //system("sh ext_skel " . implode(" ",
    $argv));
26
27  $extname = "";
28  $skel = "skeleton";
29  foreach($argv as $arg) {
30          if (strtolower(substr($arg, 0, 9)) ==
    "--extname") {
31                  $extname = substr($arg, 10);
32          }
33          if (strtolower(substr($arg, 0, 6)) ==
    "--skel") {
34                  $skel = substr($arg, 7);
35          }
36  }
37
38  $fp = fopen("$skel/skeleton.dsp", "rb");
39  if ($fp) {
40          $dsp_file = fread($fp,
    filesize("$skel/skeleton.dsp"));
41          fclose($fp);
42
43          $dsp_file = str_replace("extname",
    $extname, $dsp_file);
44          $dsp_file = str_replace("EXTNAME",
    strtoupper($extname), $dsp_file);
45          $fp = fopen("$extname/$extname.dsp",
    "wb");
46          if ($fp) {
47                  fwrite($fp, $dsp_file);
48                  fclose($fp);
49          }
50  }
51
52  ?>
```

Code Fragment 77: Source of the ext_skel_win32.php script.

The required change is to comment out line 25 of the script. Line 25 makes a system call to run the *ext_skel* script, but since you have already done this on a unix system, this step is uneccesary. You should run the script from within the Cygwin environment for simplicity. You must update some environment variables before running the script. An example of using this script (for the GLPK extension) is shown below:

```
1  export PATHEXT=$PATHEXT';.PHP'
2  export
   PATH=$PATH':/cygdrive/c/php/source/php-
   4.3.2/release_ts/cli'
3  cd /path/to/php_source/ext
4  /path/to/php.exe ext_skel_win32.php -
   extname=glpk
```

After doing this, a new file *extname.dsp* will be found in the *extname* directory. This is the Visual C++ project file required to build your custom extension. For reference, line 1 of the above steps adds the **.PHP** extension to the **PATHEXT** environment variable as required by the note in line 13 of the *ext_skel_win32.php* script (see Code Fragment 77). Line 2 adds the full path of the *php.exe* binary to the **PATH** variable within the Cygwin environment. You will modify this line to reflect the actual location of *php.exe* on your system.

You are now ready to build your extension into a Windows DLL. Open the project file in Visual C++. You may need to edit your library dependencies (if you are linking against an external library, for example) or other build flags before building your project. In the case of the GLPK project, for example, it is first necessary to build the GLPK library on windows and then add the *glpk.lib* file to the list of linker dependencies.

I also recommend changing the ouput file name of the project. By default, the output file name is *extname.dll* whereas the typical file name for a dynamically loadable extension for PHP on Windows is *php_extname.dll*. You can make this change by selecting the **Settings** menu item from the **Project** menu and then by selecting the **Link** tab. The *Output file name* can be directly edited (see Figure 6).

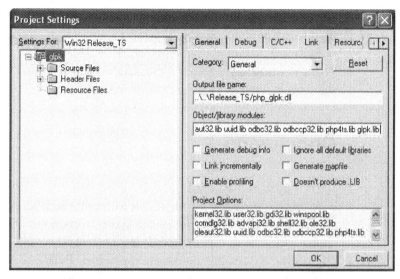

Figure 6: Changing the output file name of the extension.

You can now build your extension. The resulting DLL file must be copied to the directory specified by the *extension_dir* parameter in your *php.ini* file. Once this has been done you can have the extension loaded by PHP at startup by specifying the new DLL file in the extensions section of your *php.ini* file.

If your extension DLL statically links in its own dependencies, you need nothing more to begin testing your extension on Windows PHP. If your extension DLL requires any other external DLLs, you will need to make sure that those DLLs are located in the DLL search path.

Summary

Building extensions on Windows is slightly more complicated than building under a unix, but if you plan to redistribute your extension to the PHP community, you will likely need to provide a Windows port. The goal of this section was to show that this is a relatively straightforward process.

Conclusion

PHP is designed and has been designed from the beginning to provide a robust extension mechanism. Though not all of this functionality is documented thoroughly, the authors of PHP have obviously considered extension building a key part of PHP development and have therefore provided powerful tools for building the framework of a new extension.

This document has been an attempt to provide details for developing new extensions, customizing existing extensions and understanding the internals of PHP development. If you have questions or comments about this document, please visit the forums at http://www.php4devguide.com/.

All reasonable efforts will be made to provide updates to this document based on changes to the PHP internals and based on feedback from readers. If you feel that there is something significantly lacking in this document or if there are errors, please contact me via email at blake@intechra.net.

The source code for all the examples in this document can be downloaded from http://www.php4devguide.com/.

Appendix A: Table of Figures

Appendix B: Table of Tables

Appendix C: Table of Example Code

Appendix D: Table of Output from Examples

Index

www.ingramcontent.com/pod-product-compliance
Lightning Source LLC
Chambersburg PA
CBHW051237050326
40689CB00007B/949